English and Verbal Reasoning

Assessment Practice for the CEM test

Ages 8–9   Year 4

Michellejoy Hughes
with additional material by Jane Cooney

Great Clarendon Street, Oxford OX2 6DP

Oxford University Press is a department of the University of Oxford.
It furthers the University's objective of excellence in research, scholarship,
and education by publishing worldwide. Oxford is a registered trade mark
of Oxford University Press in the UK and in certain other countries

Text © Michellejoy Hughes 2023
Illustrations © Oxford University Press 2023

The moral rights of the authors have been asserted

All rights reserved. No part of this publication may be reproduced,
stored in a retrieval system, or transmitted, in any form or by any
means, without the prior permission in writing of Oxford University
Press, or as expressly permitted by law, by licence or under terms
agreed with the appropriate reprographics rights organization.
Enquiries concerning reproduction outside the scope of the above
should be sent to the Rights Department, Oxford University Press,
at the address above.

You must not circulate this work in any other form and you must
impose this same condition on any acquirer

British Library Cataloguing in Publication Data
Data available

978-0-19-277976-2

10 9 8 7 6 5 4 3 2 1

Paper used in the production of this book is a natural, recyclable
product made from wood grown in sustainable forests.
The manufacturing process conforms to the environmental
regulations of the country of origin.

Printed in China

Acknowledgements

Additional material by Jane Cooney

Page make-up: Integra
Cover illustrations: Lo Cole
Illustrations: Beehive Illustration

Although we have made every effort to trace and contact
all copyright holders before publication this has not been
possible in all cases. If notified, the publisher will rectify
any errors or omissions at the earliest opportunity.

Contents

Welcome 4
A Note for Parents 5
How to Use This Book 6

Learning Papers

Comprehension 8
Words in Context 13
Missing Letters 16
Vocabulary 18
Grammar 1 20
Antonyms and Synonyms 23
Grammar 2 27
Cloze 30
Curveball Questions 1:
Comprehension: Inference 32

Mixed Papers

Mixed Paper 1 36
Mixed Paper 2 42
Mixed Paper 3 48
Mixed Paper 4 52
Curveball Questions 2:
Words in Context: Homophones & Homographs . . 57

Test Papers

Test Paper 1 58
Test Paper 2 67

Keywords 76
11+ Study Guide 78
Answers A1
Progress Chart A10

Two further Mixed Papers are available online at www.bond11plus.co.uk

Welcome

The CEM Select Entrance Assessment is a computer-based 11+ test that assesses a child in verbal, non-verbal and mathematical reasoning. It covers English and maths topics that a child will be familiar with from the National Curriculum, but, in common with other 11+ exams, supplements these with verbal reasoning and non-verbal reasoning questions. What makes the CEM exam different from other assessments is the way that it blends English and verbal reasoning in one test and then maths and non-verbal reasoning in another, rather than offering four separate tests. CEM (Centre for Evaluation and Monitoring) do not offer their own practice materials or past papers and deliberately vary the contents of the exam each year, which means that the CEM 11+ is often seen as being more challenging to prepare for.

All Bond 11+ materials are effective preparation for CEM Select and develop the skills and aptitudes that a child needs for success, but CEM-specific titles, like this one, are designed to hone the flexibility of approach essential to overcoming the particular challenges of the CEM test. The Bond system provides learning, information and consolidation so that children have an extended, rich education. Our aim is to familiarise children with the type of questions they will find in the exam and to give them the transferable skills that will allow a child to attempt any question in any exam.

Bond offers a complete, flexible programme of preparation materials that you can adapt to your child's specific needs and to the requirements of the exam, or exams. There are timings provided for each section. Children can complete a paper in one sitting, using the overall timings, or in smaller timed sections. The CEM online exam has an additional 25% time allowance for candidates needing additional support. If this applies to your child, add an extra 25% for each timed section.

Why Use a Book to Prepare for an Online Test?

Since 2022, the CEM Select 11+ test has only been offered as a computer-based assessment. Whilst it is worth spending some test-practice time using an online platform such as Bond Online to gain familiarity with completing assessments through a digital interface, books remain a highly effective way of developing the skills necessary for success in a structured way whilst reducing screen time.

Not Just for the CEM Select 11+

This book has been designed to be especially effective preparation for the rigours of the CEM 11+ test, but the skills can be applied to any 11+ exams or independent school entrance exams and are also great for engaged pupils looking for an extra challenge or to ready themselves for secondary school.

Remember to keep checking in with your school of choice so that you know which exam they use – schools do change their exam boards from time to time. If your exam board does change, all is not lost. This book will still have been good preparation for other exam boards.

KEY STUDY SKILLS

Working towards an entrance exam can be an exciting challenge. It is the chance to learn new things and to prepare for secondary school. Here are some tips to help you:

- Create a study schedule so that you have a regular routine.
- Balance short bursts of practice with longer assessment papers.
- Create a quiet study space with pencils, an eraser, paper for working out, your books and a notebook for copying strategies in. If you study in different places, keep everything in a box that you can take with you.
- Write down strategies to solve new topics, but don't forget to revise and consolidate.
- Limit distractions such as television, technology and games when you are studying.
- Remember that errors are useful. They are part of the journey to success.

A Note for Parents

Parents have a crucial role in helping children and motivating them. Here are some ways that you can really make a difference.

- Check your child is working at the right level. The goal is being able to score 85% on average. It's demotivating if they can't complete questions. It is also important that they work through the system so that they are at the right level for the exam at the right time.
- Mark work promptly and go through errors. If papers have not been marked, a child has no idea how they are doing or whether they are repeating the same mistake.
- Use the Bond Handbooks to help your child understand new techniques.
- Limit the range of homework you give your child. The best results are achieved by a system that gradually increases in difficulty. Completing lots of books and papers doesn't guarantee your child's success and often creates stress.
- If your child is struggling with something specific, add additional support in that area. If your child is not achieving an 85% average in CEM-specific books you can also use other subject-specific Bond Assessment Practice books at the same level or Bond 10 Minute Tests for consolidation.
- Communication is key. Remain positive and encourage your child to focus on the positive. No exam is going to ask for 100% so pushing for that is unrealistic and stressful.
- If your child is constantly struggling, be realistic over whether a selective education is the right choice for your child now. Many children move to a selective school for their GCSEs or A levels so not going to a selective school now doesn't mean they never will. It is about finding the best school for your child.

How to Use This Book

This book includes many step-by-step techniques for solving different question types. If further support is needed it can be used alongside one or more of the Bond Handbooks, which offer insights into the full range of questions that might occur in the exam.

- The first section of the book is the Learning Papers that focus on key skills with worked examples then lots of questions for consolidation.
- The second section of the book is Mixed Papers so that children continue to consolidate and do not forget what they have learnt. Go online at www.bond11plus.co.uk and register for free resources to get two additional Mixed Papers.
- The final section includes two full Test Papers, which can be broken down into shorter sections for more focussed practice, or can be used as full mock tests for that all-important exam practice.
- There is an 11+ study guide at the back of the book with some useful hints and tips.
- There are fully worked out answers to explain how an answer has been reached.

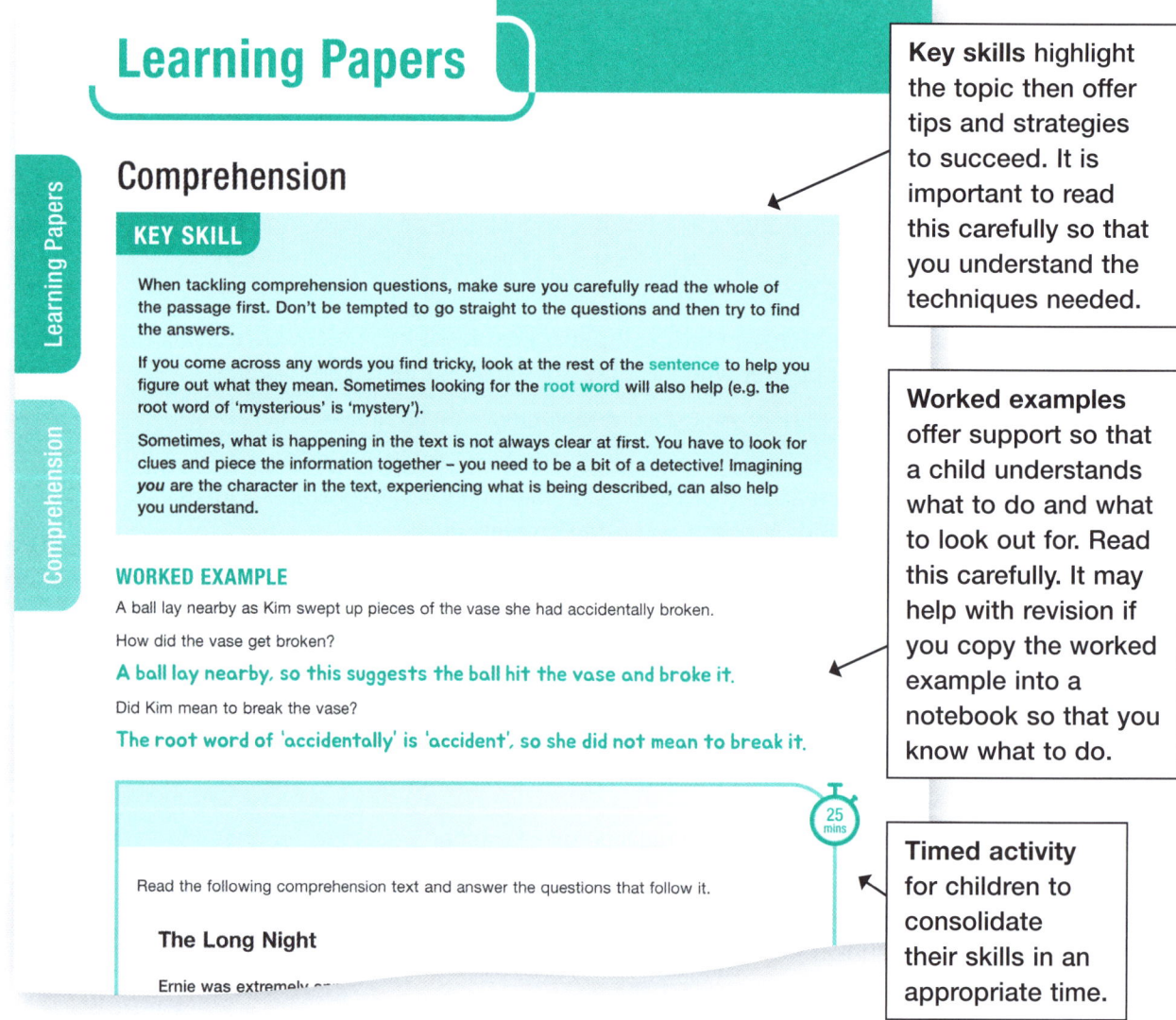

Key skills highlight the topic then offer tips and strategies to succeed. It is important to read this carefully so that you understand the techniques needed.

Worked examples offer support so that a child understands what to do and what to look out for. Read this carefully. It may help with revision if you copy the worked example into a notebook so that you know what to do.

Timed activity for children to consolidate their skills in an appropriate time.

KEY ENGLISH AND VERBAL REASONING SKILLS

The Bond English and Verbal Reasoning Book covers the elements that are found in the CEM online 11+ exam, but is useful for all CEM-style online and written 11+ exams. The Learning Papers cover the following key skills:

- **Comprehension** – a wide range of text styles, genres and question types.
- **Grammar** – including word classes, root words/prefixes/suffixes and literary effects.
- **Vocabulary** – including antonyms, synonyms, cloze exercises, spellings and words in context.

The Mixed Papers ensure the key skills are consolidated thoroughly then the Test Papers give children the opportunity to get used to the exam process as a natural progression of each book. Don't forget that a rounded education is key. Read as much as you can, play word games, do wordsearches and crosswords, create a vocabulary notebook of words that you don't know and include antonyms and synonyms whenever you can – Bond have a set of Flashcards to help make this more fun. Try solving logic puzzles – Bond also have a book that you might enjoy. Create an ongoing list of unfamiliar words and their meaning, to extend vocabulary.

Each book is part of the Bond system with books increasing gradually in difficulty. Once your child has completed this book, there is a clear progression in starting the next book level if your child has an average of 85% in this book. If they have achieved an average of 70% – 85%, then another book at the same level as this one will provide further support. If your child has achieved less than a 70% average, then moving down a level will be most useful. Once your child has developed the skills needed at a lower level, they can move up with confidence.

Learning Papers

Comprehension

KEY SKILL

When tackling comprehension questions, make sure you carefully read the whole of the passage first. Don't be tempted to go straight to the questions and then try to find the answers.

If you come across any words you find tricky, look at the rest of the sentence to help you figure out what they mean. Sometimes looking for the root word will also help (e.g. the root word of 'mysterious' is 'mystery').

Sometimes, what is happening in the text is not always clear at first. You have to look for clues and piece the information together – you need to be a bit of a detective! Imagining *you* are the character in the text, experiencing what is being described, can also help you understand.

WORKED EXAMPLE

A ball lay nearby as Kim swept up pieces of the vase she had accidentally broken.

How did the vase get broken?

A ball lay nearby, so this suggests the ball hit the vase and broke it.

Did Kim mean to break the vase?

The root word of 'accidentally' is 'accident', so she did not mean to break it.

Read the following comprehension text and answer the questions that follow it.

The Long Night

Ernie was extremely annoyed. Father Christmas had asked everyone to work overtime to make sure everything was ready for the Long Night.

Ernie was known for being a lazy elf and he was hoping to go home early so that he could have a really nice, long sleep. Ernie wondered what job he would be asked
5   to do. He didn't want to end up with a rubbish task, so if he managed to get to the back of the queue, he thought, then the other elves would have to do the worst jobs and his job would be to help another elf or even to go home early. In fact, if he was slow enough, Santa might not even see him. Ernie cheered up at this thought and when Santa asked for all of the elves to line up, Ernie made sure that he shuffled
10 unhurriedly to the back of the line.

8

1 How had Ernie planned to spend the night?

....

....

....

2 What was Ernie's plan to avoid being given a job?

....

....

Santa looked around at the elves and then down to his list of jobs. "Well, my elves," Santa boomed, "I need three helpers to box up the jigsaws, five elves to package the dolls and teddy bears, six others to put the toy cars into boxes and I need four elves to count the building blocks."

15 Ernie was thrilled that he didn't have these jobs to do. He hated boxing up as it required a lot of concentration to count properly and he always ended up with paper cuts.

Santa ticked off the first eighteen elves and off they dashed. Santa looked at the remaining eager faces. "I now need fifteen helpers to wrap the boxes up in the most
20 Christmassy of wrapping papers."

Ernie was so relieved that he didn't have to wrap up the presents. This was such a boring job and Ernie usually ended up with more sticky tape on him than on the presents. No, this was not a job that he fancied.

3 Why did Ernie not want to box up presents? Give two reasons.

....

....

....

....

4 Why did Ernie not want to wrap up presents? Give two reasons.

....

....

....

....

[2]

Santa ticked off the fifteen elves and looked at the remaining queue. "Well, my elves,
25 I need two helpers for each reindeer to wash and feed Comet, Cupid, Blitzen, Vixen,
Dasher, Dancer, Prancer, Donner and Rudolph." Santa ticked off each elf as they all
trundled off to find their reindeer.

Ernie was ecstatic! He hated washing down the reindeer as he would get soapy and
wet and they were such messy eaters that he would end up with hot oats and bits of
30 carrot all over his hands. Ernie shivered. "What a gross job that is!" he thought. Ernie
counted the remaining elves. Including himself there were just fourteen left.

Santa counted the remaining elves. "Well, my elves, I now need three helpers to
polish the sleigh and to make sure that it's ready for the Long Night. I then need
another ten elves to load up all of the boxes into sacks and then onto the sleigh. It is
35 such an important job and needs great care and attention."

The chosen elves giggled, so pleased to be given such an important job. Ernie giggled
to himself, glad to be left. Who wants to carry heavy boxes to and fro and be too hot
indoors and too cold outdoors? No, this was no job for Ernie. He was above this.

Santa ticked off the remaining job and then turned to find Noel Claus, when out of the
40 corner of his eye, he saw a movement behind the Christmas tree. "Ernie. Is that you?"
asked Santa.

5 Why did Ernie not want to wash and feed the reindeer? Give two reasons.

....

....

....

....

[2]

6 Why did Ernie not want to clean and pack the sleigh? Give two reasons.

....

....

....

....

....

7 How did Santa notice Ernie?

....

....

....

....

Ernie scowled. He was so annoyed that he had been spotted.

"Well, Ernie, I have all of my jobs ticked off, so let me think what else needs doing." Santa rubbed his chin, pulling gently on his long white beard. Then all of a sudden
45 Santa looked at his pocket watch and then turned to Ernie triumphantly. "Ernie. I know exactly what job would be good for you!"

Ernie looked at Santa, feeling sure that the job would be doing something pointless like tying the ribbons on the dolls' hair or making sure there were batteries in the toys.

"Ernie. The reindeer will have eaten by now and need someone to shovel up any
50 mess they have made. They have to feel comfortable before their long travels, so go and grab a shovel, a brush and a bucket and when you have collected all of the reindeer dung, pop it all in the Christmas garden compost heap. We'll all have some lovely roses in the summer."

Ernie was horrified. To his dismay he had the worst job. In fact, this job was the worst
55 possible job in the whole wide world. Ernie plodded to the stables and looked at the floor. What a mess! Cold oats, bits of carrot, lots of straw and now loads of steaming reindeer dung. Ernie was going to have a very, VERY, **VERY** Long Night.

8 How would Ernie help the reindeer feel if he completed this task?

....

9 What did tools did Ernie need to complete the task he was given?

....

....

10 What would the reindeer dung be used for?

....

....

.... [1]

11 Find two words or phrases in the last paragraph which tell us how Ernie felt about the task he had been given.

....

.... [2]

12 What do these words mean as used in the text? Provide a definition.

   a unhurriedly (line 10)

      ....

      .... [1]

> **TOP TIP!**
> Practise scanning: looking quickly through the text to find a particular word or part of a story. This will help you to find information more quickly and easily.

   b eager (line 19)

      .... [1]

   c ecstatic (line 28)

      .... [1]

   d dismay (line 54)

      .... [1]

13 Give three ways the author uses the word 'very' in the last sentence.

....

....

.... [3]

Total: 25

> **TOP TIP!**
> Read as much as you can – books, magazines, and instructions. Research a favourite topic or hobby on the internet. This will help build up your vocabulary and make comprehension much easier.

Words in Context

KEY SKILL

When you have to choose a word to fit into a sentence, read the whole sentence first. It may give you clues as to what the word could be.

If you are unsure of the meaning of some words, cross out the ones you know are definitely incorrect first. This will leave you with fewer options to choose from and help you find the correct answer more easily.

WORKED EXAMPLE

Complete each sentence by selecting the best word from the options **a**, **b**, **c**, **d** or **e**.

We saw a **cow** when we went to the dairy farm.

a	b	c	d	e
walrus	cow	shark	whale	jellyfish

The sentence is about a visit to a dairy farm, so think about what one is and what you would find there. 'Walrus', 'shark', 'whale' and 'jellyfish' are all sea creatures, so they must be incorrect and can be crossed out. This leaves us with the correct answer, which is 'cow'.

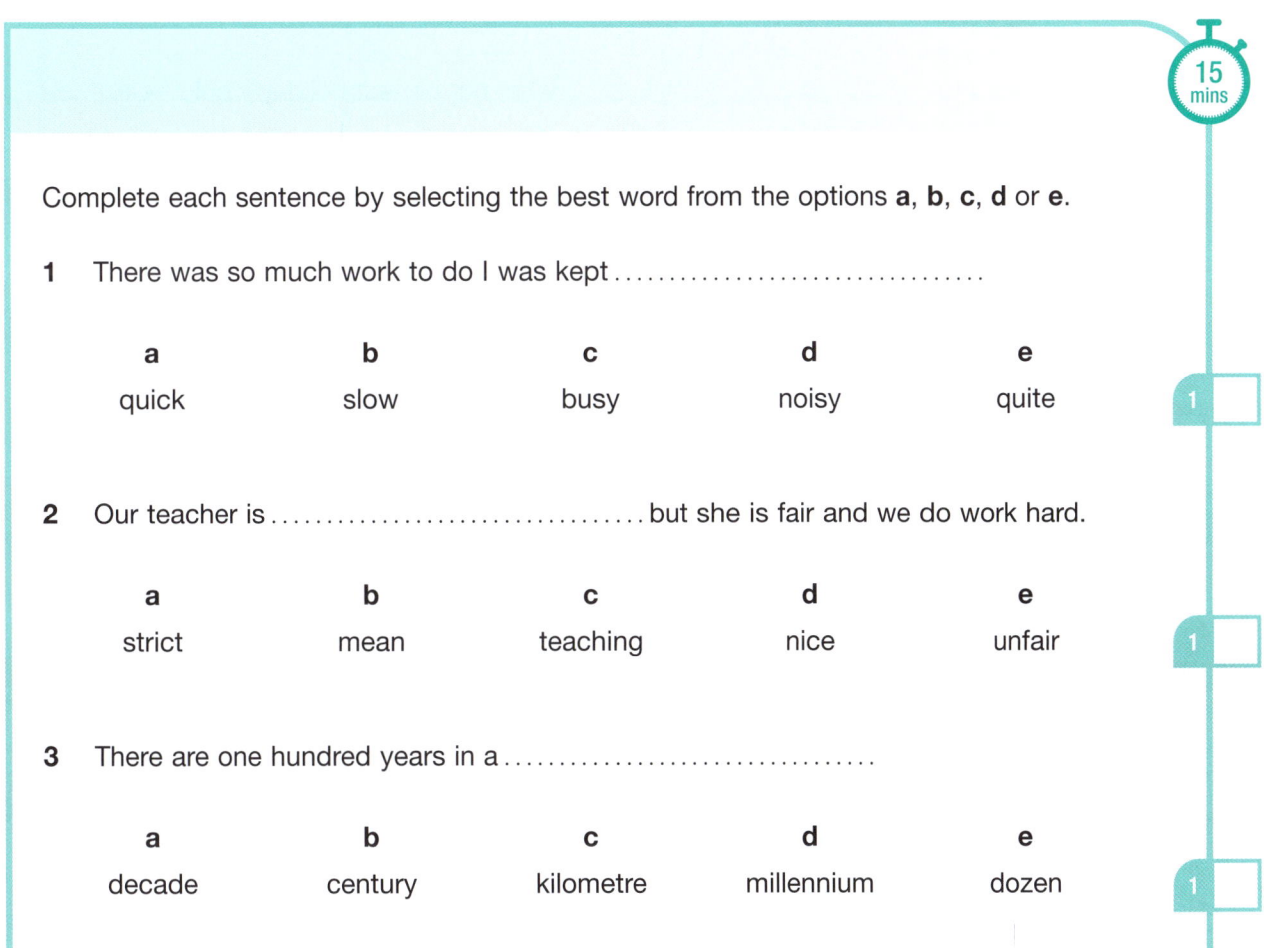

Complete each sentence by selecting the best word from the options **a**, **b**, **c**, **d** or **e**.

1   There was so much work to do I was kept ....

a	b	c	d	e
quick	slow	busy	noisy	quite

2   Our teacher is .... but she is fair and we do work hard.

a	b	c	d	e
strict	mean	teaching	nice	unfair

3   There are one hundred years in a ....

a	b	c	d	e
decade	century	kilometre	millennium	dozen

> **TOP TIP!**
> Read the sentence aloud to yourself, with your chosen word inserted. Sometimes words that are similar to the correct answer are among the options, but do not sound right. Don't be caught out!

4 I took the .... that the doctor had prescribed.

a	b	c	d	e
medicine	drink	food	question	nurse

5 There was a large .... of girls at the park.

a	b	c	d	e
group	litter	pack	herd	flock

6 The .... dog dragged the clean clothes from the washing line.

a	b	c	d	e
sleeping	friendly	sensible	brave	naughty

7 We were asked to .... what our perfect holiday would be like.

a	b	c	d	e
talk	imagine	remember	prefer	visit

8 Michael likes a .... of fruit such as pears, berries and bananas.

a	b	c	d	e
library	spoon	variety	few	select

9 To bake this cake we need to .... the egg white from the yolk.

a	b	c	d	e
desperate	exaggerate	separate	multiply	add

10 In Brownies we made our .... to serve our community.

a	b	c	d	e
promise	threat	shout	cry	question

WORKED EXAMPLE

Read the following sentences and answer the questions. Underline the correct answer.

'I am going to start writing a story.' What does the word 'start' mean?

a	b	c	d
stop	pen	**begin**	continue

'Stop' is the opposite of 'start' and 'continue' means to carry on, so these can be crossed out. Although 'pen' and 'tale' are connected with story-writing, the sentence will not make sense if they are inserted. This leaves option c, so 'begin' is the correct answer.

Read the following sentences and answer the questions. Underline the correct answer.

11 'We meet every Wednesday and occasionally on a Friday night.' What does 'occasionally' mean?

a	b	c	d
party	never	always	sometimes

12 'We have a dog to guard our house.' What does 'guard' mean?

a	b	c	d
protect	find	betray	entertain

13 'What is that peculiar smell?' What does 'peculiar' mean?

a	b	c	d
beautiful	horrible	strange	sweet

14 'Perhaps we will go to the library later.' What does 'perhaps' mean?

a	b	c	d
promise	maybe	definitely	doubtful

15 'I feel sick, therefore I won't go to the park.' What does 'therefore' mean?

a	b	c	d
so	and	but	because

Words in Context

Missing Letters

KEY SKILL

If you find this type of question tricky, develop your knowledge of **letter patterns**. These are groups of letters often found together in words, for example, 'igh', 'ough' or 'tch'. They can also be **prefixes** (which are found at the beginning of a word) or **suffixes** (which are found at the end of the word). Examples of prefixes are: 're', 'dis' and 'pre'. Examples of suffixes are: 'tion', 'ing' and 'ful'.

WORKED EXAMPLE

Find the three letters that complete these words. The three letters do not have to make a word.

g a r d **e n i** n g

Start with the easiest letter to solve first: when 'ng' is found at the end of a word, the letter 'i' is often before it to form 'ing'. This gives us 'gard_ _ing', making it easier to find the remaining letters. Think of two letters that can go next to one another after 'gard': the letters 'en' will give us the word 'garden', therefore the word must be 'gardening'.

Find the three letters that complete these words. The three letters do not have to make a word.

1 ord _ _ _ ry   _ _ _ ncess

2 pun _ _ _ ed   donk _ _ _

3 _ _ _ derful   brin _ _ _ g

4 tea _ _ _ rs   stoc _ _ _ gs

5 p _ _ _ aps   po _ _ _ ar

6 r _ _ _ bow   c _ _ _ ken

7 _ _ _ erstood   borr _ _ _ d

8 som _ _ _ mes   any _ _ _ re

9 darl _ _ _   fi _ _ _ ork

TOP TIP!
Have fun writing silly poems! Words that rhyme often have the same letter patterns, so this will help you become familiar with more spellings.

KEY SKILL

When a sentence includes a shortened word in capitals, always read the whole sentence first. It will give you clues as to what the missing letters might be.

WORKED EXAMPLE

Find the three-letter word that can be added to the letters in capitals to make a new word. The new word will complete the sentence sensibly.

I was out of BRH after running for the bus. **EAT**

The sentence is describing something that happens after running. As you are 'out of breath' after running, the word in capitals must be 'BREATH'. You can then circle or underline the letters you have added to find the three-letter word: BR<u>EAT</u>H.

TOP TIP!
Write out the whole word to see if it looks right, as the way you pronounce some letters may change.

Find the three-letter word that can be added to the letters in capitals to make a new word. The new word will complete the sentence sensibly.

10 The twins needed to behave TSELVES. ....

11 I have a new pen for WRIG with. ....

12 The wind was BING strongly. ....

13 The sun was behind me casting long SOWS. ....

14 Grandma makes lovely sticky toffee PUDG. ....

15 That star is the BHTEST in the sky. ....

Total 15

Vocabulary

KEY SKILL

To find words which are the odd ones out, eliminate the two words that do not fit with the other three. Try to find three words that are connected and check that they have the same connection. The remaining two words are the odd ones out.

WORKED EXAMPLE

Underline the two odd words out in the following group of words.

pentagon   octagon   *pencil*   hexagon   *table*

Begin by comparing 'pentagon' to each of the other words: 'pentagon', 'octagon' and 'hexagon' are all shapes. 'Pencil' and 'table' are left and neither have anything in common with the other words, so they are the odd ones out.

⏱ 18 mins

Underline the two odd words out in the following groups of words.

1	kitten	puppy	giraffe	elephant	hippopotamus
2	nose	mouth	eyes	fingers	toes
3	rice	plate	pasta	bowl	dish
4	hear	walk	ears	legs	talk
5	earring	bracelet	necklace	gold	silver
6	cottage	town	village	city	house
7	forest	woods	poppy	daisy	sunflower
8	snail	butterfly	worm	moth	slug
9	nostrils	brows	lips	lashes	lids

KEY SKILL

Some questions involve finding a word that has two meanings. Begin by comparing the first word shown in the brackets to each pair of words. If it only matches one pair, cross it out. Repeat this with the other words in the brackets until you find the answer.

WORKED EXAMPLE

Underline the one word in brackets that goes equally with both pairs of words.

see, notice   dot, speck   (look, stain, watch, **spot**)

Begin by checking the word 'look' against both pairs of words. Although it can mean 'see' and 'notice', it does not mean 'dot' or 'speck', so cross it out. Repeat this with each of the other words in brackets. Only the word 'spot' can mean 'see' or 'notice' *and* 'dot' or 'speck', so this is the answer.

TOP TIP!

If you find these types of questions tricky, read through each of the words again and ask yourself if any of them could be pronounced differently. For example, the word 'close' can mean 'nearby' but when pronounced differently it can also mean to 'shut'.

Underline the one word in brackets that goes equally well with both pairs of words.

10 clever, brainy   light, shining   (dull, bright, intelligent, gleaming)

11 walks, paces   stairs, ladders   (rope, plods, steps, marches)

12 call, telephone   circle, loop   (ring, buzz, disk, doughnut)

13 rigid, strong   difficult, tough   (inflexible, stiff, firm, hard)

14 cruel, nasty   stingy, miserly   (kind, lovely, mean, bad)

Total 14

Grammar 1

> **KEY SKILL**
>
> Some questions will ask you to change **plural** words to **singular**. To help answer these questions, remind yourself of the spelling rules about plurals. For example:
>
> - 'es' is added to words ending in 's', 'ss', 'sh', 'ch', 'x' or 'z'
> - when a word ends in 'y', this letter is removed and 'ies' is added and so on.

WORKED EXAMPLE

Write the singular version of these words in these **sentences**.

The **wolf** (wolves) pup leapt around playfully in the grass.

Most of the time 's' or 'es' just needs to be removed to make a word singular. However, in this case, we get 'wolve' or 'wolv' and neither looks right. If this happens, look at the letter before 's' or 'es'. As this is a 'v', the letter 'f' will have been removed and replaced with 'ves'. Therefore the answer is 'wolf'.

Write the singular version of these words in these sentences.

1 Lil lives in a .... (houses) with a blue door.

2 There is a .... (churches) at the end of our street.

3 Only one .... (children) scored top marks.

4 Trevor has a new .... (scarves) to wear in the cold weather.

5 We've had our dog since he was a .... (puppies).

6 There is a .... (flies) in my drink.

7 Brooke has her .... (lunches) at school.

KEY SKILL

For questions where the words in a sentence are muddled up, read the muddled sentence aloud first. It sometimes helps to ignore words such as 'a', 'an' and 'the', as there will be fewer words to order. Focus on the **nouns** and **verbs** to get an idea of what the sentence could be about.

WORKED EXAMPLE

Rearrange these words to make the longest sentence you can.
Underline the one word that is not needed.

car   raced   around   a   <u>mouse</u>   the   track.   **A car raced around the track.**

Once 'a' and 'the' have been removed, we are left with: 'car', 'raced', 'around', 'mouse' and 'track'. Only the words 'car', 'raced', 'around' and 'track' would make sense together in a sentence, so 'mouse' must be the extra word and needs to be underlined. Then try different combinations of the remaining words. The most sensible option would be describing a 'car' that 'raced' 'around' a 'track', so rewrite the sentence in this order, inserting the 'a' and 'the' that were removed.

TOP TIP!
Don't worry if you don't find the correct order the first time – lots of children find this type of question tricky. Just keep trying different orders until you find the answer.

Rearrange these words to make the longest sentence you can. Underline the one word that is not needed.

8   In   a   cinema   are   circus   artists   trapeze.

....

9   The   leg   wagged   his   little   dog   tail.

....

10   The   bakery   had   no   Vikings   about   the   books   library.

....

11   Handbag   queen   gold   wore   crown   her   the.

....

12   Five   divide   three   add   two   makes.

....

KEY SKILL

Questions that involve conjunctions can be tricky, as some will work in some sentences but not others. Think about *why* the conjunction is being used: if it is to add more information, words like 'and' or 'also' are used. If it is to add an explanation, words like 'because' or 'as' are used.

WORKED EXAMPLE

Take a different **conjunction** from the box and place it in a space so that each **sentence** makes sense.

or	because	although

We were allowed to have a longer playtime **because** our class won the writing competition.

Read the whole sentence first to get an idea of what it is about. Then read the sentence aloud with a different word from the box inserted each time. 'Because' makes the most sense, as the words that follow it explain *why* they were allowed to have extra playtime.

TOP TIP!

Remember that each word in the box can only be used once. If you get stuck on a question, look to see if you have already used a possible answer in a previous sentence.

Take a different **conjunction** from the box and place it in a space so that each **sentence** makes sense.

because	but	or	so	yet

13 Kayleigh was reading a book .... she should have been putting her toys away.

14 Jodie was tired .... she went to bed late last night.

15 Would you like an orange .... would you prefer an apple?

16 He is ten now .... he is old enough to know better.

17 That film is my favourite .... I've never seen the sequel.

Total: 18

Antonyms and Synonyms

KEY SKILL

A **synonym** is a word that has the same or similar meaning to another word. For example, 'small' is a synonym of 'little'.

An **antonym** is a word that has the opposite meaning to another word. For example, 'loud' is the antonym of 'quiet'.

If you come across any words you find tricky, ask yourself if you have heard or read them anywhere before. Ask yourself questions like these:

- How were they used in the **sentence**?
- What was it describing?

It can also help to think of your own sentences using the word shown in the question. You can then replace it with other words you can think of that have a similar or opposite meaning, to help find the answer.

WORKED EXAMPLE

| large | jolly | huge | computer | enormous |

Find three words that are synonyms of the word 'big'.

large, huge, enormous

Think of a sentence with the word 'big' in. For example:

'I didn't realise how big dinosaurs were until I saw a skeleton at the museum!'

Try replacing 'big' in the sentence with each of the words shown, one by one. Look for words that keep the meaning of the sentence the same. Only 'large', 'huge' or 'enormous' can be used in this way, therefore they are all synonyms of 'big'.

Look at the following words and then use them to answer the questions that follow.

sow	claw	borrow	howl	burst
yell	nail	scream	freezing	clean
deal	field	rather	trade	young
safe	cooler	cheer	grief	spotless
sparkling	plant	chilly	harmless	icy

1 Find three words that are **synonyms** for the word 'cold'.

....

....

2 Find two words that are **antonyms** for the word 'dangerous'.

....

....

3 Find three words that are **synonyms** for the word 'shout'.

....

....

4 Find three words that are **antonyms** for the word 'dirty'.

....

....

5 Find two words that are **synonyms** for the word 'talon'.

....

....

Look at the following words and then use them to answer the questions that follow.

taste	kind	reveal	loss	expose
build	arch	shut	meal	fright
dread	trying	defeat	flame	make
spy	fear	frog	create	hammer
soft	horror	band	flying	mild

6 Find two words that are **antonyms** for the word 'win'.

....

....

7 Find three words that are **antonyms** for the word 'destroy'.

....

....

8 Find two words that are **antonyms** for the word 'hide'.

....

....

9 Find four words that are **synonyms** for the word 'terror'.

....

....

10 Find three words that are **synonyms** for the word 'gentle'.

....

....

WORKED EXAMPLE

Add the missing letters to the word on the right to make a word with the most similar meaning to the word on the left.

happy   ch __e__ __e__ rf __u__ l

Put the word on the left into a sentence of your own. For example:

'She was feeling very happy as she had won the prize.'

Think of words that can replace 'happy' in the sentence. For example, 'jolly', 'cheerful' or 'merry' all have the same meaning. Only the letters from the word 'cheerful' fit, therefore this is the answer.

Add the missing letters to the word on the right to make a word with the most similar meaning to the word on the left.

11 pants   t __ o __ s __ r __   1

12 hot   b __ r n __ __ g   1

13 entire   w __ o __ e   1

14 share   __ i __ i __ e   1

15 sound   n __ __ se   1

WORKED EXAMPLE

Underline the one word on the right that has the most opposite meaning to the word on the left.

small   tiny   little   angle   <u>giant</u>   pen

Read through all the words and cross out any that you are sure cannot be correct. 'Tiny' and 'little' have the same meaning, so can be crossed out. 'Angle' and 'pen' do not have anything to do with the word 'small', so can also be crossed out. This leaves 'giant', which is the opposite of small and therefore the correct answer.

> **TOP TIP!**
> Always check whether you are being asked to find the synonym or the antonym in the question. This type of question can ask for either.

Underline the one word on the right that has the most opposite meaning to the word on the left.

16	**important**	vital	main	irrelevant	key	strict
17	**whole**	complete	part	central	finished	ended
18	**often**	rarely	frequent	many	few	always
19	**answer**	reply	regret	exclaim	question	write
20	**catch**	drop	crawl	fall	net	problem

Total **37**

Grammar 2

> **KEY SKILL**
>
> Some questions will ask you to find **homophones**. These are words that sound the same but have a different spelling and meaning. For example, 'heal' and 'heel' both sound the same, but 'heal' means to get better and 'heel' is a part of the foot. Learn as many homophones as you can: not only will it help with your spelling, but it will help build your vocabulary too!

WORKED EXAMPLE

Underline the one homophone in each line.

boat   <u>plane</u>   car   lorry   helicopter

Look at each word in turn and ask yourself if you have heard the word used in any other way. Also ask yourself if you have read a similar word anywhere, but with a different spelling. All the words are types of transport, but only 'plane' can be written differently. When it is spelled 'plain', it means 'not decorated'.

A homophone is a word that sounds like another but has a different spelling. Underline the one homophone in each line.

1	red	yellow	green	orange	black
2	cod	haddock	plaice	salmon	halibut
3	latest	new	fresh	ripe	young
4	cover	clothe	conceal	wear	blanket
5	three	five	seven	two	nine
6	drank	ate	swallowed	chewed	devoured

(25 mins)

KEY SKILL

If you are asked to find and fix misspelt words, thinking of spelling rules will help. Ask yourself questions like these:

- Do any letters need to be doubled?
- Should any letters change when a **suffix** is added?
- Are the **letter patterns** shown (e.g. 'eigh' or 'ough') correct?

WORKED EXAMPLE

Write out the misspelt words in the right-hand box, so that the spellings are correct and the **sentence** makes sense.

The teecher read a thriling story to her class.

1 **teacher**

2 **thrilling**

TOP TIP!
If you complete the easiest spellings first, make sure you write your answer next to the correct question number!

Look at each word in turn, thinking about if any other letter patterns have the same sounds as the ones shown. In the word 'teecher', the 'ee' sound can also be written as 'ea'. Rewrite it with these letters so you can see if it looks correct. Also think about **root words**. For example, 'ing' has been added to the root word 'thrill'. However, when it is removed from the word shown, we are left with 'thril', which looks incorrect.

7–14 The underlined words in this paragraph have not been spelled correctly. Write out the misspelt words in the right-hand box, so that the spellings are correct and the paragraph makes sense. The first word has been done for you.

To make a Sorrento Smoothey you need the folowing ingredients: ten strawberys, two appels, one bannaanna, two peaches (take the stones out), two scoowps of vannilar ice cream and one litre of milk. Blend the frute and milk together in a liquidiser to make the smoothie base. Pour half of it into a tall glass, add the ice creem and top up with the rest of the smoothie base.

e.g. **smoothie**

7 ....

8 ....

9 ....

10 ....

11 ....

12 ....

13 ....

12 ....

14 ....

KEY SKILL

Some questions may be about the **tense**, which tells us when something happened. To change the tense, look at the **verb** or **verb phrase** in the sentence, for example in the sentence 'I am hopping', the verb phrase is 'am hopping'.

To change the sentence into the past tense, most **verbs** will just need to have 'am' removed, and 'ing' changed to 'ed'. For instance, 'am hopping' would become 'hopped'. However, some sentences may contain **irregular verbs**, like the example below, where the whole word changes instead.

WORKED EXAMPLE

Put these **sentences** in the **past tense** using the smallest number of words possible.

I am eating a sandwich.   **I ate a sandwich.**

The past tense of 'eat' is 'ate', therefore 'ate' replaces the **verb phrase** 'am eating'.

'I was eating' would not be correct, as the question asks you to use the smallest number of words possible.

Put these sentences in the past tense using the smallest number of words possible.

15 I am riding my bike.

....

16 Megan is speaking to Grandma.

....

17 Liam is washing his hair.

....

18 We are running in the race.

....

19 Katie is writing in her diary.

....

20 My mum is driving her new car.

....

Total **20**

Cloze

> ### KEY SKILL
>
> When tackling cloze questions, where you have to fill spaces in a paragraph, read through the words in the box and the whole paragraph first, to get an idea of what it could be about.
>
> Insert any words you are certain of. This will leave fewer words to choose from for the rest of the question, making it easier.
>
> Look for clues in the sentences to help put the remaining words in the right places.
>
> If you find any words tricky, check to see if they have another meaning. For example, 'right' can mean the opposite of left, or it can mean correct.
>
> Also think about words that are often written together, for example 'post office'.
>
> Finally, read through the whole paragraph with the words you have inserted to check it makes sense.

WORKED EXAMPLE

Put the words in the box into the correct place in the paragraph below.

thrilled	right	studying	hard

Will had always found maths challenging, but worked **hard** and felt good when he got the questions **right**. He had spent a lot of time **studying** for the latest test and was nervous about his result. Finally, his teacher handed out the marked answer sheets to everyone and he was **thrilled** to see that he had got every question correct. All his hard work had been worth it!

As the words 'worked' and 'hard' often go together, 'hard' must be the first word. The next part of the sentence is describing what made Will feel good about the questions. Although 'right' has two meanings, in this case it means 'correct' and is the second word. For the third word, Will is described as doing something for the test. As you study for tests, 'studying' is the next word. This then leaves 'thrilled', which is the fourth word.

> ### TOP TIP!
> **Cross out the words in the box as you insert them – this will make it easier to see which ones are left. Make sure you do this in pencil though, in case you make a mistake!**

1–10 Put the words in the box into the correct place in the paragraph below.

| animals | emerged | finding | hopped | hunted |
| lived | squirrel | twitching | undergrowth | vixen |

In the woods there .... many .... such as the grey ...., who spent each day busily rushing around .... nuts from the trees then burying the nuts here and there. The rabbits .... about .... their whiskers as they played. At night, the nocturnal animals came out. The .... and her fox cubs .... for food as the black and white badgers .... from their sett snuffling and stomping in the ....

11–15 Put the words in the box into the correct places in the paragraph below.

| distance | looking | planets | remember | telescope |

There are eight planets in our solar system. In order of .... from the sun, the .... are Mercury, Venus, Earth, Mars, Jupiter, Saturn, Uranus and Neptune. I use this sentence to .... the order of them: **M**y **V**ery **E**arly **M**orning **J**og **S**hould **U**pset **N**obody. All of these planets can be seen with binoculars or a .... and some can even be seen just by .... up to the sky.

Curveball Questions 1

Comprehension: Inference

Sometimes a comprehension text can be tricky to understand as it is not always immediately clear or obvious what a writer is describing. When this happens, you have to look for clues and piece the information together – you have to be a bit of a detective! This sounds trickier than it is, so don't worry, just think of it as a puzzle to be solved.

Begin by practising figuring out what is being described in the following sentences.

WORKED EXAMPLE

What am I? I am one of the maths operations, but also look like a letter.

x

The maths operations are: +, –, x and ÷. The symbol 'x' looks like the letter 'x', so this is the answer.

⏱ 8 mins

1. What am I? I am often called a king, even though I am not human. Hear me roar!

   ....

2. What am I? You pack me to take on a school trip so you don't go hungry!

   ....

3. What am I? I am a juice that has the same name as my colour.

   ....

4. What am I? I usually only come out at night, but don't scare me into a prickly ball!

   ....

Next, try figuring out what is being described in *groups* of sentences. Sometimes it helps to imagine *you* are the character in the text, experiencing what is being described. It can also help to keep asking yourself the following: **who** is it about?; **where** is it taking place?; and **when** is it taking place?

WORKED EXAMPLE

She quickly uncoiled the hose from the red truck to help put out the fire. Meanwhile, her colleague climbed the ladder to rescue a boy who was waving frantically from a window.

Who is being described and what is she doing?

A firefighter. She is helping to rescue a boy from a fire.

We know this because the first sentence tells us she is uncoiling a hose from a red truck: fire engines have hoses on them to put out fires and they are red. The second sentence tells us her colleague (someone she works with) is rescuing someone, which is what a firefighter's job is.

---

5 Although Marcus thought it was fun having his friends sign the plaster cast on his leg, he decided he was definitely going to be more careful the next time he played rugby!

What has Marcus done and how did he do it?

....

....

6 Mei-Lin can't wait for school to finish today! As it isn't a school day tomorrow, she is going to a sleepover at her friend's house.

How is Mei-Lin feeling and what day of the week is it?

....

....

7 She had spent all afternoon at the river without getting a single bite on her line. Suddenly, she felt a tug on the rod and prepared to reel it in, excited to see what she had caught.

What is she doing and why is she excited?

....

....

Logic problems

WORKED EXAMPLE

Read the following paragraph and then answer the questions that follow.

On Sports Day the green and yellow team won a different match each. One team won the egg-and-spoon race and the other team won the tug-of-war. Joshua's team won the tug-of-war and Evie's team won the egg-and-spoon race. Yuxuan was in the green team and Otto was in the yellow team. Evie was in the same team as Otto.

What was the colour of Joshua's team? **Green**

Read through the question to get an idea of what it is about. Pick out the information you need to put in a table, like the one shown, putting ticks in the boxes as you go.

We know Joshua took part in the tug-of-war and Evie took part in the egg-and-spoon race, so tick these boxes. We know the colour of Yuxuan and Otto's teams, so tick these boxes as well. Evie was in the same team as Otto, which means she must have been in the yellow team. This means that Otto was in the team that won the egg-and-spoon race. We now also know that Joshua and Yuxuan were in the green team, which won the tug-of-war.

	Egg-and-spoon	Tug-of-war	Green	Yellow
Joshua		✓	✓	
Evie	✓			✓
Yuxuan		✓	✓	
Otto	✓			✓

Read the following paragraph and then answer the questions that follow.

Four little kittens are very playful. Topsy has a red collar and white paws, and her sister Flopsy has a blue collar and black paws. The youngest kitten, Tipsy, has black paws and a red collar and the oldest kitten, Dipsy, has the same colour paws as Topsy and the same coloured collar as Flopsy.

8 Which kitten has a red collar and black paws?

   ....

9 Which kitten has a red collar and white paws?

   ....

10 Which kitten has a blue collar and white paws?

    ....

11 Which kitten has a blue collar and black paws?

    ....

Mixed Papers

Mixed Paper 1

Read the following comprehension text and then answer the questions that follow it.

Pals of the Parrotfish

The huge parrotfish is over a metre long and can change its colour from the brightest blues and greens to pinks, oranges and yellows. It has lots of teeth that are tightly packed together, making its mouth look like a parrot's beak. These teeth allow it to munch away at coral and rock, as well as the occasional little fish.

5   Parrotfish can form a protective layer when they go to sleep at night, but as this mucus layer is brightly coloured, it looks as though the parrotfish is wearing pyjamas! Although parrotfish look pretty and amusing to us, they must look very scary to other fish and that is where their little mates come in.

    The goby fish is less than 10 centimetres long, although some species are less
10 than 10 millimetres long, making them some of the smallest fish in the world. These peaceful little fish are sometimes called the 'cleaner' or 'doctor' fish for one clever reason. When the big parrotfish has eaten well, its teeth get full of food that begins to rot. How would your teeth feel if you never brushed them? Well, this is how the parrotfish feels, but it doesn't have a toothbrush or toothpaste. What the parrotfish
15 does have is the tiny goby.

    The parrotfish swims up to the little goby and shows its buddy that there is no danger of being eaten. The little fish swims up to the giant parrotfish's mouth and swims in and out, nibbling at the rotten flesh of the parrotfish to keep it healthy and gobbling up the food that is stuck to the parrotfish's teeth until they are as clean as a new pin.

20 The parrotfish leaves with nice clean teeth and no rotting flesh. The goby has a tummy full of food without having to go and hunt for it. The parrotfish and the goby both need each other to work together in harmony.

TOP TIP!

Always check the text to make sure you get the correct answer – don't just rely on memory.

1   What are the three words used in the extract that mean the same as 'friend'?

    ....

    ....

2   How do you think the parrotfish gets its name?

    ....

    ....

3   Why does the mucus layer make the parrotfish look like it is wearing pyjamas?

    ....

4   When and why does the parrotfish form a mucus layer?

    ....

    ....

5   Why do you think the goby fish is called the 'cleaner' or 'doctor' fish?

    ....

    ....

6   Can you find a **simile** in the fourth paragraph?

    ....

7   What do these words mean as used in the text? Provide a **definition**.

    a   munch (line 4) ....

    b   tummy (line 21) ....

    c   firm (line 22) ....

8 Give two reasons why the parrotfish and goby need each other.

....

.... [2]

Grammar

Rearrange these words to make the longest **sentence** you can.
Underline the one word that is not needed.

Example   car   raced   around   a   <u>mouse</u>   the   track.

A car raced around the track.

⏱ 7 mins

9 Wash your feet before need to sandwiches making you hands.

.... [1]

10 The garden shed we planted a rose in bush.

.... [1]

11 Denim are often wood made jeans from.W

.... [1]

12 The space was running bus to late town.

.... [1]

13 The boats returned with full coaches fishermen.

.... [1]

Take a different **conjunction** from the box and place it in a space so that each **sentence** makes sense.

| or | because | although |

Example We were allowed to have a longer playtime **because** our class won the writing competition.

| although | because | but | if | or | so |

14 Joe loves to eat lasagne.....................he doesn't like pizza.

15 Yasmin is not eating lunch.....................she is fasting.

16 Philip was hungry.....................he ate a sandwich.

17 Dad said that I could go out on my bike.....................I could go shopping with him.

18 ....Connor was angry with his sister, he didn't lose his temper.

19 I can come to your house for a playdate.....................your mum calls mine.

Words in Context

Read the following **sentences** and answer the questions. Underline the correct answer.

Example 'I am going to start writing a story.' What does the word 'start' mean?

| a | b | c | d | e |
| stop | pen | begin | continue | tale |

20 'I need to blend the ice cream with the fruit.' What does 'blend' mean?

a	b	c	d
beat	separate	mix	make

21 'All pupils need to form a queue behind their class teacher.' What does 'queue' mean?

a	b	c	d
circle	line	choir	group

22 'Mum wants a career as a teacher.' What does 'career' mean?

a	b	c	d
conversation	meeting	child	job

23 'We live in the south-east region of the country.' What does 'region' mean?

a	b	c	d
area	county	country	village

Grammar

Write the **singular** version of these words in these sentences.

Example   The <u>wolf</u> (wolves) pup leapt around playfully in the grass.

24 Mum placed the .... (cushions) on the bed.

25 There was no money left in Mina's .... (purses).

26 The .... (thieves) stole the boy's scooter.

27 We had a .... (parties) to celebrate Grandpa's birthday.

28 The .... (mice) nibbled the cheese.

Cloze

Put the words in the box into the correct place in the paragraph below.

right	hard

Example Will had always found maths challenging, but worked
<u>hard</u> and felt good when he got the questions <u>right</u>.

29–33 Put the words in the box into the correct place in the paragraph below.

climb	bear	ears	eat	hours

The panda is a type of .... found in China. With its white face and

black eyes and ...., it looks very different from other bears. Not

only can pandas ..... trees, but they can swim as well. Although you may know they mainly

.... bamboo shoots, you might be surprised to learn that they

spend over 10 .... a day eating!

Mixed Paper 2

Grammar

Put these **sentences** in the **present tense**.

Example   Sammy toasted a sandwich.
    Sammy toasts a sandwich.

Most **verbs** will just need 'ed' removed and 's' added. For instance, 'toasted' becomes 'toasts'. However, some sentences may have **irregular verbs**, so more letters in the word may change. For example, the present tense of 'flew' is 'flies'.

1 Bella drew a picture.

....

2 Simon climbed the ladder.

....

3 The dog slept in his basket.

....

4 Kayleigh drove the tractor.

....

5 Erica flew a kite.

....

6 Pneuma thought about a holiday.

....

Write out the misspelt words in the right-hand box, so that the spellings are correct and the sentence makes sense.

The <u>teecher</u> read a <u>thriling</u> story to her class.

1 **teacher**

2 **thrilling**

7-14 The underlined words in this paragraph have not been spelled correctly. Write out the misspelt words in the right-hand box, so that the spellings are correct and the paragraph makes sense. The first word has been done for you.

The <u>cannall</u> seems such a <u>peacfull</u> place doesn't it? Yet if you sit beside the water and keep <u>queite</u> and still, you would certainly change your mind. Little water rats zoom here and there, water voles and tiny shrews busy <u>themselevs</u> as vivid <u>colord</u> kingfishers fly to and from their nest. Ducks, swans and a whole host of <u>insexts</u> live off the water. A canal is <u>actuly</u> a very busy <u>habbittatt</u> and a wonderful place for <u>naychur</u> to thrive.

e.g. **canal**

7 ....

8 ....

9 ....

10 ....

11 ....

12 ....

13 ....

14 ....

8

Vocabulary

Underline the one word on the right that has the most similar meaning to the word on the left.

Example   simple   different   single   difficult   <u>easy</u>   eager

Read through all the words and cross out any you are sure cannot be correct. 'Different', 'single' and 'eager' do not have anything to do with the word 'simple', so can be crossed out. 'Difficult' means the opposite, so can be crossed out as well. This leaves 'easy', which can replace 'simple' in a sentence, so it is the correct answer.

TOP TIP!

Increase your knowledge of homophones. These are words that sound the same, but have different spellings *and* meanings. For example, 'sea' is a large body of water and 'see' means to view with the eyes.

Underline the one word on the right that has the most similar meaning to the word on the left.

15	**dressed**	talked	home	residence	clothed	wardrobe
16	**centre**	shape	circle	edge	middle	side
17	**thought**	idea	brain	spoke	knew	ignorance
18	**possess**	danger	prohibit	stop	own	pay
19	**probably**	impossible	definitely	maybe	never	always

TOP TIP!

Develop your knowledge of homographs. These are words that have the same spelling but have different meanings, e.g. the word 'right' can mean the opposite of left *or* something that is correct.

Underline the one word in brackets that goes equally with both pairs of words.

Example   see, notice   dot, speck   (look, stain, watch, spot)

Underline the one word in brackets that goes equally well with both pairs of words.

20	bat, wickets	party, prom	(racquet, ball, jig, owl)
21	coop, hutch	pencil, crayon	(kennel, barn, pen, paint)
22	glue, attach	pole, rod	(paste, stick, connect, post)
23	cute, adorable	dessert, pudding	(lovely, sweet, kind, poppet)
24	pill, medicine	laptop, notebook	(tablet, lotion, computer, smart)
25	overturn, spill	tearful, weepy	(knock, cry, upset, mean)

Comprehension

Read the following comprehension text and answer the questions that follow it. It is a tricky extract so read slowly and use the titles of each section to help you. The titles of each section will help you.

The Kings and Queens of England

Normans (1066–1154)
When William the Conqueror (William I) won the Battle of Hastings in 1066, he became the first Norman king. After William, the country was then ruled by William II, Henry I, Stephen and finally Matilda. We place the roman numerals after the name of each king
5 or queen to mean William the first or William the second, otherwise people would not know which William we mean. There are still Norman building styles in England and the Normans also gave the English language many new words.

Plantagenets (1154–1399)
King Henry II was the first of the Plantagenet kings followed by Richard I, John I, Henry III,
10 Edward I, Edward II, Edward III and Richard II. The Plantagenet kings gave us a parliament, some very violent wars abroad and fighting in England, while Wales was conquered.

House of Lancaster (1399–1461)
Henry IV took the throne from Richard II to begin the dynasty we refer to as the House of Lancaster. After Henry IV, Henry V and Henry VI ruled. Henry VI was only nine months
15 old when he became king, but he remained king until he was in his thirties. In 1455, the famous 'Wars of the Roses' began between the houses of Lancaster and York.

House of York (1461–1485)
King Edward IV was the first king from the house of York. He was followed by Edward V and Richard III. When Edward IV died, the crown passed to Edward V who was only 12,
20 but he ended up as one of the young princes who were locked in the Tower of London and never seen again. Richard then became heir to the crown although most people suspect that he was involved in the deaths of the two young princes.

The Tudors (1485–1603)
Richard III died in battle and Henry VII took the crown. After Henry VII, England was
25 ruled by Henry VIII, Edward VI, Lady Jane Grey, Queen Mary I and finally Elizabeth I. During the Tudor period, England became a huge colonial power. During this time, Wales and England were united through an Act of Union. Henry VIII was well known for his many wives, whereas Lady Jane Grey was only queen for nine days and was beheaded when she was only 17.

30 ### The Stuarts (1603–1649 then 1660–1714)
James I was the first of our Stuart kings. He was followed by Charles I, Charles II, James II, William III, Mary II and Anne. In 1649, king Charles I was killed and England was left without a king. Instead no monarch ruled, although Oliver Cromwell took charge between 1653 and 1658. Charles II took over in 1660 to continue the Stuart
35 period. In 1707, England and Scotland were united by another Act of Union.

House of Hanover (1714–1901)

King George I was the first Hanoverian King of England. He was followed by George II, George III, George IV, William IV and Queen Victoria. This was a German line of monarchs who ruled us after Queen Anne had died without leaving any children. King George was her closest Protestant relative. During this period of time, another Act of Union united Great Britain with Ireland.

Saxe-Coburg-Gotha and the Windsors (1901–present day)

King Edward VII was the first king after Queen Victoria. After him, the United Kingdom was ruled by George V, Edward VIII, George VI, Elizabeth II and Charles III. When George V took to the throne, there was a lot of anti-German feeling because of the First World War, so he changed the family name to Windsor.

26 Why do you think William I was also known as William the Conqueror?

....

....

27 Why do we use the Roman numerals after each king or queen's name?

....

....

28 Who was the first Plantagenet king?

....

29 When did the Wars of the Roses begin? ....

30 Who was the last king of the House of Lancaster?

....

31 How old was Edward V when he was made king?

....

32 How many queens were there in the Tudor period?

....

33 Who was beheaded at the age of 17?

....

34 Who was the third king in the Stuart period?

....

35 For how long did Oliver Cromwell rule? ....

36 In what period of time was the first Act of Union?

....

37 In what period of time was Great Britain united with Ireland?

....

38 Who was the last Hanoverian monarch?

....

39 Why were we ruled by a German line of royal family?

....

40 Why did the Saxe-Coburg-Gotha change their name to Windsor?

....

Mixed Paper 3

Comprehension

Read the following comprehension text and answer the questions that follow it.

Charlie and Me

Charlie is my favourite friend,
We go everywhere together.
He makes me laugh, he makes me smile,
We'll be friends forever.

5   I have fair hair, he has brown.
He always smiles, I often frown.
He is always trying to cheer me up,
When I am feeling down.

Last year we both went camping,
10 A site beside the sea,
We watched the stars, we heard the waves,
As happy as could be.

We visited a castle, the beach
And a hilltop zoo,
15 We laughed so much together
As we usually do.

To find a friend like Charlie,
I know is really rare.
Charlie is my favourite friend,
20 He's my oldest teddy bear.

1   What type of creature is Charlie?

....

2 Find three examples that show us this is a poem.

....

....

....
[3]

3 Which four places does Charlie visit?

....

....

....
[4]

4 The word 'site' (line 10) is a **homophone** with the word 'sight' because they sound the same but have different spellings and a different meaning. Can you find another word in the same **stanza** that is also a homophone?

....
[1]

5 Which one phrase is repeated?

....

....
[1]

6 Find three ways in which Charlie is such a good friend.

....

....

....
[3]

7 The words 'we will' are joined with an apostrophe to make 'we'll' in the first stanza. This is called a **contraction**. Which two words are joined together in the same way in the last stanza?

....
[1]

Missing Letters

Find the three-letter word that can be added to the letters in capitals to make a new word. The new word will complete the **sentence** sensibly.

Example   I was out of BRH after running for the bus.

BR<u>EAT</u>H   <u>EAT</u>

8   With a new moon, the night is DER than usual. ....

9   Today in school we LNT about the Tudors. ....

10   Have you BORED my red crayon? ....

11   Would you RAR have grapes or an apple with your cheese? ....

12   Root vegetables include carrots, swedes and TIPS. ....

13   People that we do not know are called STGERS. ....

14   My friends enjoy roller SKAG but I keep falling over! ....

TOP TIP!
It helps to write out the whole word, as the way some letters are pronounced changes sometimes.

Vocabulary

Underline the two odd words out in the following groups of words

Example   purple   lilac   <u>olive</u>   <u>sage</u>   violet

15	huge	big	tiny	little	small
16	magazine	book	newspaper	television	radio
17	freezing	icy	boiling	hot	cold
18	heart	hand	liver	elbow	kidney
19	car	coach	bus	driver	passenger
20	milk	yoghurt	cheese	bread	cake

Antonyms and Synonyms

Add the missing letters to the word on the right to make a word with the most similar meaning to the word on the left.

Example happy   ch <u>e</u> <u>e</u> r f <u>u</u> l

21 wash   c __ __ an

22 ill   __ o __ r __ y

23 heat   wa __ __ __ h

24 big   __ __ __ ge

25 tall   h __ __ h

26 style   f __ s __ i __ n

27 cut   sn __ __

A homophone is a word that sounds like another word but has a different spelling. Underline the one **homophone** in each line.

Example boat <u>plane</u> car lorry helicopter

28 wring   squeeze   twist   spin   rotate
29 view   sight   vision   spot   picture
30 beard   moustache brush   hair   extensions
31 them   those   think   their   thought
32 sheep   horse   donkey   cow   goat
33 break   holiday   vacation trip   escape

Mixed Paper 4

Antonyms and Synonyms

4 mins

1	**accidental**	clumsy	deliberate	dangerous	mistaken	occasion
2	**certain**	unsure	sure	insure	reassure	assure
3	**increase**	include	creased	shrink	grow	large
4	**minute**	second	hour	tiny	huge	medium
5	**ordinary**	plain	expected	reduced	normal	unusual

Words in Context

Underline the correct words in each of these **sentences**.

Example: She (<u>blew</u>, blue) her trumpet solo in the school (<u>band</u>, banned)

Even if you are unsure of some of the spellings shown, by focusing on the words you *are* familiar with you can still work out the correct answer. For example, you may know the word 'blue' means a colour, but you may be unsure of what 'blew' is. The colour 'blue' wouldn't make sense in the sentence, therefore the other word must be the correct answer.

8 mins

Underline the correct words in each of these sentences.

6   There are lots of (poor, pour) countries in the (whirled, world).

7   Sometimes there is a lack of (rain, rein) or too much (son, sun).

8 Sometimes farmers cannot grow enough food, or (their, there) country may (be, bee) at war.

9 In some countries people (die, dye) when their most basic (kneads, needs) are not met.

10 We don't have to (know, no) someone to care (for, four) them.

11 When we (raise, rays) money, we help to (safe, save) the lives of other people.

Grammar

Rearrange these words to make the longest **sentence** you can. Underline the one word that is not needed.

Example: car raced around a mouse the track.

A car raced around the track.

TOP TIP!
If the sentence includes the words 'the', 'a' or 'an', they will always go before a **noun** or an **adjective + noun**.

12 The hurricane gently bobbed the flowers in pretty breeze.

13 As a lemon our cherry car as new is red.

14 Robert working loved museum the displaying at.

15 The two were enemies of best friends the children.

WORKED EXAMPLE

Write out the **root word** for each of these words.

unhappiness   *happy*

Look for any prefixes (such as 're', 'pre', 'un', 'in' and 'im') and any suffixes (such as 'tion', 'ly', 'ies' and 'ed'). Remove these from the word to help find the root. For example:

unhappiness = un + happi + ness

Taking them out gives us 'happi', but it doesn't look correct. When this happens, check whether the end of the root word has been changed so that a suffix can be added. In this case, the 'y' in 'happy' was changed to an 'i' before 'ness' was added.

Write out the root word for each of these words.

16 magically ....

17 beautiful ....

18 silliness ....

19 cleverest ....

20 smaller ....

Vocabulary

Underline the two odd words out in the following group of words.

Example: pentagon   octagon   <u>pencil</u>   hexagon   <u>table</u>

21	twenty	fifteen	thirty	nineteen	sixty
22	pentagon	shape	angle	octagon	hexagon
23	autumn	leaves	winter	snow	summer
24	couple	one	pair	double	single

54

Missing Letters

Find the three letters that complete these words. The three letters do not have to make a word.

Example: g a r d **e n i** n g

25 lad ___ ___ ___ rd   d ___ ___ ___ ionary

26 n ___ ___ ___ hty   li ___ ___ ___ acy

27 ___ ___ ___ wded   show ___ ___ ___ ng

28 ___ ___ ___ embly   lem ___ ___ ___ de

Put the words in the box into the correct place in the paragraph below.

| right | hard |

Example: Will had always found maths challenging, but worked **hard** and felt good when he got the questions **right**.

29–34 Put the words in the box into the correct place in the paragraph below.

| decorations | neighbour | birthday | arrived | games | ready |

Lily was so excited – it was finally the day of her ………… party! She looked around the room to check everything was ………… The cake her ………… had made sat proudly in the centre of the table, prizes for the ………… were tucked in the corner and there were ………… everywhere! Suddenly, the doorbell rang. The first guest had …………!

Finished these Mixed Papers? Go online at **www.bond11plus.co.uk** and register for **FREE RESOURCES** to get two additional Mixed Papers.

Curveball Questions 2

Words in Context: Homophones and Homographs

Sometimes a homophone or homograph of the correct answer may be included as one of the possible options in a question. Familiarise yourself with these types of words so that you are not caught out!

Remember:

Homophones are words that sound the same but have a different spelling and meaning.

Homographs are words that have the same spelling but have different meanings.

Each question below shows three homophones and their definitions. Some words are also homographs, which means that particular spelling has more than one meaning, so both definitions are shown wherever this is needed. Draw a line to match each word to its correct definition. Make sure you look carefully at how each word is spelled and, if you are unsure of any words, use a dictionary to help.

7 mins

1	a	aisle	The shortened form of the words 'I will'
	b	isle	A corridor or walkway
	c	I'll	A small island
2	a	by	Spoken when you leave somebody
	b	bye	A word used to show who does something *or* another word for 'next to'
	c	buy	Get something by paying money
3	a	there	Used to describe a place or position
	b	their	The shortened form of the words 'they are'
	c	they're	Used to describe something that belongs to a person or group of people
4	a	to	to Another word for 'so that' or 'toward'
	b	too	The number that comes after one
	c	two	Another word for 'as well'
5	a	pore	Low quality *or* having no money
	b	pour	To carefully tip liquid
	c	poor	A tiny hole in the skin

6	a	road	The past tense of 'ride'
	b	rode	A tarmac track that cars drive on
	c	rowed	Moved a boat with oars

WORKED EXAMPLE

Read the following **sentence** and then find two examples of each word class to complete the table below.

The hungry man sat down and ate his delicious dinner, quickly and greedily.

noun	man	dinner
verb	sat	ate
adjective	hungry	delicious
adverb	quickly	greedily

As noun is a person, place or thing, 'man' and 'dinner' must be the nouns.

Verbs are 'action' words, therefore 'sat' and 'ate' are the verbs.

Adjectives describe nouns. The man is described as 'hungry' and the dinner is described as 'delicious', so these are the adjectives.

Adverbs describe verbs and often ends in 'ly'. The way the man is described as eating is 'quickly' and 'greedily', so these are the adverbs.

Read the following **sentence** and then find two examples of each word class to complete the table below.

The little owl looked carefully at the tasty food before screeching loudly.

7	noun		
8	verb		
9	adjective		
10	adverb		

Test Papers

Test Paper 1

Read the following comprehension text and then answer the questions that follow it.

The Great Under-12 Cook Off Show

In this week's edition we are looking ahead to the new *The Great Under-12 Cook Off Show* and share a lovely recipe from last year's winner. Don't forget to complete the crossword on page 24 and send it to us by March 15th as one lucky winner will get a copy of Samuel Jacobson's new recipe book. Here at the *Great Under-12 Cook Off Show*, we're excited about the new series. There are twelve programmes in the series that we will be treated to. Here is the full series so that you don't miss any of your favourites.

Date	Theme	Description
5th May	Cakes	From coffee to toffee – all of our favourite big cakes.
12th May	Bakes	Little cakes, flapjacks and lunchbox favourites.
19th May	Biscuits	Spiced, iced, savoury and sweet biscuits.
26th May	Breads	Rolls, batches, baps and loaves.
2nd June	Scones	Sweet, savoury and drop scones.
9th June	Muffins	From healthy breakfast muffins to cupcakes and fairy cakes.
16th June	Occasions	Weddings, birthdays and all manner of decorated cakes.
23th June	Tarts & Pies	From tiny jam tarts to huge tarte tatins, this will test our bakers.
1st July	Puddings	Sponges, steamed puddings and fruit crumbles.
8th July	Final	Our winner is announced after a show-stopping cake finale.

To kick off the show, we're going to share some top tips and a winning recipe from last year's winner, Samuel (Sammy) Jacobson, interviewed by Tope Oyeyemi.

"Hey Sammy - it's been nearly a year since your win, so how was your year?"

"I cannot tell you how exciting it was to take part and then to win. It has been a mad year as I have been in school during the week and then at the weekend, I've been doing cookery demonstrations and writing my first cookery book aimed at children."

"Wow, Sammy, that sounds so busy! Would you recommend our readers take part in the competition?"

"I know that filming has finished for this year, but they will soon be looking for new participants, so sign up and take part because it will change your life. It was the best thing that I have ever done."

"Finally Sammy, can you give us a tasty recipe out of your new book?"

"Of course! Here is my recipe for easy autumn crumble with a healthy twist and a top tip."

"Many thanks, Sammy, and we'll all be cheering on this year's contestants!"

Next week Tope Oyeyemi will be interviewing Cupcake King Chitavake Kumar with some ideas on how to decorate your cupcakes so that they look professional.

Sammy's Super Sweet Crumble

Ingredients for the filling:

500 g autumn fruit such as apples, plums, pears, blackberries (either one fruit or mixed)

75 g sugar

25 g butter

$\frac{1}{4}$ teaspoon of mixed spice or cinnamon (if you fancy it; if not, miss it out)

$\frac{1}{4}$ teaspoon of dried chilli (I know it sounds mad, but trust me, it works perfectly)

Ingredients for the crumble topping:

100 g plain flour

250 g porridge oats (coarse, fine, a mixture of the two – it doesn't matter)

200 g butter, cut into chunks

180 g brown sugar (white if you don't have brown)

Method:

Preheat the oven to 180°C/Gas Mark 4.

1. Throw all of the filling ingredients into a saucepan and heat through gently until the fruit is soft enough to place a fork through it. Apples are dense and will take 10 minutes, but softer fruit like plums will only take 2 minutes.

2. Fling all of the crumble topping ingredients into a clean bowl and use a fork to stir it all up together and to spread the butter throughout the topping.

3. Chuck the fruit mix into your oven-proof bowl.

4. Toss the crumble topping on top of the fruit and pop it in the oven for 45 minutes.

5. Serve with custard, cream or ice cream.

> **TOP TIP!**
> You can make up loads of crumble topping, pop it in a freezer bag and freeze it. It will stay in chunks so it is easy to use. For a quick pud, grab a tin of fruit and put it in an oven-proof bowl, then tip over a few generous handfuls of crumble topping and bake.

Next week's edition comes with a free guide to making sugar paste roses. Out on Monday from all good newsagents.

1. Where would you expect to find this text? Can you find three things to back up your point of view?

   ....

   ....

   ....

   ....

   [4]

2. What date do you think you could see a ginger biscuit being made?

   ....

   [1]

3. What will be made on the 16th June?

   ....

   [1]

4. What will be the date of the final?

   ....

   [1]

5. What was the name of last year's winner of the *Under-12 Cook Off Show*?

   ....

   [1]

6. Why does the fruit take different times to cook?

   ....

   [1]

7. How much butter do you need in total to make the recipe?

   ....

   [1]

8. What do the words on the left mean as used in the text? Underline the answer.

a coarse	rough	soft	rude	smooth	flat
b participants	readers	writers	contestants	eaters	children
c twist	spiral	leap	version	plait	bunch

   [3]

9 Reread the 'Method' section of the recipe. The word 'throw' is informal. Can you find another four informal words in this section?

....

....

....

.... 4

Take a different **conjunction** from the box and place it in a space so that each **sentence** makes sense.

and	because	but	or	so

10 Lewis wanted to play ice hockey .... he joined the local team. 1

11 Sam and Spencer had a sleepover .... it was the weekend. 1

12 Mum makes lovely callaloo .... she cooks delicious pelau. 1

13 Grace prefers dogs .... Emily prefers cats. 1

14 Next year, we will go on holiday to France .... we might go to Spain. 1

Find the three-letter word that can be added to the letters in capitals to make a new word. The new word will complete the sentence sensibly.

15 The gardener was cleaning her forks and SES. ....

16 We couldn't go through the door as it had 'PRIE' on it. ....

17 The rare eagle was STED by the bird watcher. ....

18 We placed the strawberries into the BET. ....

19 Herrmann put the MITS on to keep his hands warm. ....

20 Please don't feed the EONS that flock into the city centre. ....

21 Mum put on her coat and picked up her HBAG. ....

Look at the following words and then use them to answer the questions that follow.

different	learn	notice	experience	unusual
favourite	strange	trust	island	best
reign	continue	surprise	appear	trapped
considered	undecided	purpose	reveal	unsure
caught	rule	thought	odd	govern

22 Find three words that are synonyms for the word 'control'.

....

....

23 Find four words that are antonyms for the word 'ordinary'.

....

....

24 Find two words that are synonyms for the word 'uncertain'.

....

25 Find two words that are antonyms for the word 'free'.

....

Write the plural version of these words in these sentences.

26 They bought three .... (**box**) at the craft stall.

27 The library had four .... (**copy**) of the book.

28 There were some .... (**donkey**) in the paddock.

29 The dogs were .... (**hero**) for saving the drowning lamb.

30 The autumn trees were losing their .... (**leaf**).

31 The dentist had to remove two of the girl's .... (**tooth**).

32 The fields were full of little harvest .... (**mouse**).

Read the following **sentences** and answer the questions. Underline the correct answer.

33 'At dusk the scent of the honeysuckle was at its sweetest.'

    a What does the word 'dusk' mean?

a	b	c	d
dawn	noon	sunset	midnight

    b What does the word 'scent' mean?

a	b	c	d
perfume	colour	growth	flowers

34 'The stoat danced and leapt to hypnotise the unsuspecting hare.'

    a What does the word 'leapt' mean?

a	b	c	d
turned	ran	jumped	stared

    b What does the word 'unsuspecting' mean?

a	b	c	d
shy	stationary	entertained	unknowing

35 'The war was continuing with no sign of ceasing from either side.'

    a What does the word 'continuing' mean?

a	b	c	d
fierce	slowing	ongoing	fighting

    b What does the word 'ceasing' mean?

a	b	c	d
stopping	pinching	persisting	remaining

Put these **sentences** in the **past tense** using the smallest number of words possible.

Example   I am eating a sandwich.   I ate a sandwich.

36 We are watching a film.

....

37 Simona is playing football with her friends.

....

38 Mei-Lin is practising for her piano exam.

....

39 I am making a model of a ship.

....

40 She is drawing a picture of a horse.

....

41 Thea is reading her book.

....

42 We are having a picnic.

....

43–47 The underlined words in this paragraph have not been spelled correctly. Write out the misspelt words in the right-hand box, so that the spellings are correct and the paragraph makes sense.

The first word has been done for you.

In Febuary it will be a centuary since our school was bilt. We want to make the histery of our school available for everyone to read about, so we have extended the school libary. Now anyone can come in and find out more and to help us celebrate our speshul occasion.

e.g. **February**

43 ....

44 ....

45 ....

46 ....

47 ....

A **homophone** is a word that sounds like another word but has a different spelling.
Underline the one **homophone** in each line.

Example   wish   <u>war</u>   when   wicket   welcome   (war and wore)

Underline the one homophone in each line.

48	excited	challenged	interested	engaged	bored
49	you	me	us	them	her
50	him	she	his	this	it
51	height	weight	length	breadth	width
52	tree	shrub	flower	bulb	plant

Total 70

Test Paper 2

Underline the one word on the right that has the most opposite meaning to the word on the left.

Example rose thorn flower <u>fell</u> down up

Underline the one word on the right that has the most opposite meaning to the word on the left.

1	**disappear**	vanish	go	appear	dissolve	resolve
2	**early**	first	late	start	stop	dawn
3	**difficult**	impossible	hard	soft	easy	sufficient
4	**regular**	uneven	even	often	level	ordered
5	**possible**	likely	probable	potential	unlikely	imaginable
6	**natural**	ordinary	normal	usual	expected	artificial

Find the three-letter word that can be added to the letters in capitals to make a new word. The new word will complete the **sentence** sensibly.

Example We HED the keys to the estate agent. **AND**

Find the three-letter word that can be added to the letters in capitals to make a new word. The new word will complete the sentence sensibly.

7 HVER you travel, leave plenty of time to get here. ....

8 The optician has given me some GLES to correct my sight. ....

9 The BCHES of the tree needed pruning. ....

10 Some people think that THIRN is unlucky. ....

Look at the following words and then use them to answer the questions that follow.

weak	dull	drowsy	wrecked	purse
cloth	stool	change	watch	broken
order	wise	simple	sleepy	chew
tied	ruined	roam	sure	paid
dozy	tired	sore	easy	material

11 Find three words that are synonyms for the word 'destroyed'.

....

....

....

12 Find four words that are antonyms for the word 'energetic'.

....

....

13 Find two words that are antonyms for the word 'difficult'.

....

14 Find two words that are synonyms for the word 'fabric'.

....

Add the missing letters to the word on the right to make a word with the most similar meaning to the word on the left.

Example vision   s <u>i</u> g <u>h</u> t

Add the missing letters to the word on the right to make a word with the most similar meaning to the word on the left.

15 container   c __ __ t __ n

16 fire   bla __ __

17 creature   __ __ ast

18 amount   n __ __ __ er

19 damage   in __ __ __ y

20 afraid   sca __ __ __

21 dirty   u __ __ __ __ an

Read the following sentences and answer the questions. Underline the correct answer.

22 'We are going to close the shop on a Wednesday.' What does 'close' mean?

a	b	c	d
shut	empty	nearby	front

23 'The weather last night was very pleasant.' What does 'pleasant' mean?

a	b	c	d
rainy	funny	nice	stormy

24 'After the shock of the accident she looked really pale.' What does 'pale' mean?

a	b	c	d
sad	happy	white	dark

25 'Why is the cost of that book so high?' What does 'cost' mean?

a	b	c	d
sale	price	tax	money

Write out the **root word** for each of these words.

Example   unhappiness   happy

26 resitting   ....

27 travelling   ....

28 impossibly   ....

29 inactive   ....

30 unsettled   ....

Write the singular version of the words in these sentences.

31 Would you like a .... (glasses) of milk?

32 Hera is the name of a Greek .... (goddesses).

33 The little .... (piglets) followed its mother.

34 The .... (ponies) in the field was chasing another.

35 Is there a .... (fairies) at the bottom of our garden?

36 There is a .... (people) looking for Dad.

37 Ben saw a .... (monkeys) at the zoo.

38 Raj needs a .... (knives) to cut the bread.

Read the following comprehension text and answer the questions that follow it.

The Old and the New

"Where's Al?" Mum called as she came downstairs carrying a cardboard box. "Look, I've found a whole stash of really old comics in the attic," she continued as she placed the box on the table. Al lifted the lid of the box to reveal a dazzling comic with paper as fragile as tissue. She wasn't keen on reading books, but comics were another matter.

5   Al sat flicking through the comics, mainly *Superhero Bonanza,* which contained stories and articles, when she came across a long brown envelope. The envelope had already been opened. Al said, "Look Mum, it says Cecily Hastings, 47 School Lane, Ashbury, Worcestershire. That's our address! Who is Cecily Hastings?" Mum looked up from unwrapping plates. "The people we bought the house from were called Moghi and
10 they had been here for more than thirty years so it must have been before them."
Al peered in and took out a thin piece of paper filled with spidery writing. Al soon realised, with growing excitement, that she was looking at a beautifully written letter. "Mum listen," she began, 'Rosebud Cottage, Daisy Bank, Worcestershire.' Al frowned, "Where is that?" Mum smiled. "Whenever someone writes a formal letter, they write
15 their own address at the top. That address is where the writer of the letter lives. Can you imagine a time before we could text or call someone?" Al shook her head and continued to read. "To my dearest Cecily, I am so awfully thrilled that you were able to visit last Saturday. We had such a wonderful time in the gardens and I hope that it will not be long before you are able to visit again. Next time I should love to find the
20 sunken garden that must be on the other side of the door. Nanny says that if we walk across Bluebell Field to the corner of Smestow Farm, we should be able to reach the back of the sunken garden, so we could try this."

Al looked at her mum questioningly. "Where is Bluebell Field or Smestow Farm or Daisy Bank? They all sound so pretty."

25 Mum shrugged. "I don't know, love. I'm still trying to get my bearings."

Al looked back at the letter. "Jeffrey is renovating the orangery at the manor house. I can visit him whenever I like as long as I don't disturb him. The rosebeds are now looking rather marvellous. Although it is only early June, the heady smell of honeysuckle fills the evening air and the lilac tree looks delightful. I do so wish that
30 you could be here at the moment. It is the most beautiful place in the whole world. Please ask your mama if you can ride here at the weekend and until then, toodle pip, your loving friend Gladys."

Al looked through the French doors at her new garden. "Dad, can we have a sunken garden?"

35 Dad laughed. "Al – I don't really know what one is, but you've only just got enough garden to kick the football about. Do you really want to give that up?"

Al looked back to the cardboard box and top of the pile was an old map of Worcestershire. Al reasoned that if Cecily could ride to this beautiful garden, it couldn't be that far away. She opened the map and poured over it.

40 "What have you got there?" Mum asked.

"It's just an old map," replied Al, "but I can't find any gardens on it."

"Let's have a look," Mum said. "Can you see the farm on there?" She took the map from Al and within a few minutes, She had found not only Smestow Farm, but also Bluebell Field and Daisy Bank. Mum laughed again, "Al, I don't think this is really a
45 garden as such. If it is large enough to be named on this map, I think it is more like a park!" Al was so excited. "Please Mum, can we go and find it? It isn't far away, is it?"

Mum looked at her watch. "No, it isn't far and I suppose we could have a quick drive up there now, before we finish unpacking. I must admit I am more than ready to escape from these boxes."

50 Al sat in the back of the car, feeling so excited. She could almost smell the roses and honeysuckle. She could picture the lilac tree and she was desperate to know what an orangery and a sunken garden looked like. She wondered whether he would find the garden and whether it still looked the same. Maybe now it had changed and it was a park for everyone to enjoy. Al wasn't so sure about sharing the garden with
55 everyone else, but even if it was now a park, she had something special as she had the letter.

Mum followed the little lanes cutting through the farmland until she reached a more built-up area. Dad frowned and checked the map. "How did people cope without Sat Navs?" she grumbled under her breath. "It's straight on here," she said, continuing
60 through the traffic lights. More houses and shops gradually appeared alongside the road. Al saw churches, schools, a post office, another row of shops, some offices and a multi-storey car park. Mum turned into another road even bigger than before, in an area that should have been the crossroads of Smestow Farm and Bluebell Field. Al looked in shock at what she saw.

65 There were no roses, no honeysuckle, no lilac tree, no sunken garden and nothing that looked remotely like an orangery. Before her, and sprawling back as far as he could see, were the familiar names of a retail park. The huge supermarket, the shoe warehouse, the fast food drive-through restaurants and a massive cinema stood next to a giant clothes shop, a rambling range of well-known shops and the huge neon
70 sign that declared, 'Bluebell Retail Park'.

Underline the correct letter (or letters).

39 Where was the letter?

    a on the table   **c** inside a book

    b on the top of the cardboard box   **d** in the middle of the pile of comics

40 Who lived at Rosebud Cottage?

    a Al   **c** Gladys

    b Cecily   **d** Jeffrey

41 What two reasons did Mum give for not creating a sunken garden?

    a It would be too expensive.   **c** Mum hadn't got his bearings yet.

    b It would take a long time to build.   **d** There was not enough space.

    e Al wouldn't be able to play football.

42 What two reasons did Mum give for agreeing to look for the garden?

    a It would be large enough to be like a park.

    b Mum wanted a rest from unpacking.

    c Mum wanted to get his bearings.

    d It was quite close by.

    e Mum wanted to do some shopping.

43 How do you think Al felt when they arrived at their destination?

    a excited   **c** happy

    b relieved   **d** upset

44 Why do you think Al felt like this?

    a She loved retail parks.   **c** She was expecting flowers and trees.

    b She hated shopping.   **d** There was a massive cinema.

45 What do the words on the left mean as used in the text? Underline the answer.

a	**stash**	bag	collection	parcel	chest
b	**dazzling**	delicate	old	tough	colourful
c	**renovating**	restoring	building	destroying	painting

46 How do you think Al would have felt if she had found the garden was an open park?

    a pleased so that other people could enjoy it

    b jealous as she didn't want to share the garden

    c angry as she didn't want the garden to look different

    d excited as she would love to tell people about his letter

Underline the one word on the right that has the most opposite meaning to the word on the left.

Example   rose   thorn   flower   <u>fell</u>   down   up

47	**arrive**	leave	come	entrance	part	entry
48	**believe**	trust	faith	doubt	certainly	hope
49	**fresh**	latest	new	current	old	near
50	**opposite**	parallel	near	antonym	similar	apart
51	**interested**	engaged	fun	absorbed	special	bored
52	**end**	finish	conclude	begin	continue	partial

Underline the one word in brackets that goes equally well with both pairs of words.

Example   chilly, breezy   trendy, fashionable   (cold, <u>cool</u>, warm, chic)

53	shirt, blouse	lid, cap	(jacket, outer, top, pop)
54	breeze, gust	twist, turn	(wind, gale, storm, rotate)
55	teach, coach	plane, taxi	(car, train, tutor, cab)
56	second, hour	tiny, little	(day, time, minute, dinky)
57	leap, jump	summer, winter	(bounce, autumn, spring, hop)
58	watched, viewed	slice, carve	(cut, saw, sight, glimpsed)
59	stumble, fall	outing, journey	(stagger, trip, trek, voyage)

Keywords

Some special words are used in this book. You will find them in **bold** each time they appear in the Papers. These words are explained here.

adjective	a word that describes someone or something
adverb	a word that describes an action
antonym	a word with a meaning opposite to another word, for example *wet* and *dry*
conjunction	a word that links sentences phrases or words, for example *and, because*
consonant	any letter in the alphabet that is not a vowel
contraction	two words shortened into one with the use of an apostrophe, *it is = it's*
definition	the meaning of a word
homograph	a word that has the same spelling as another word but a different meaning; for example, *watch* can mean observe or a timepiece worn on the wrist
homophone	a word that has the same sound as another but with a different meaning or spelling, for example *pain, pane*
irregular verb	a verb that changes its spelling when changed into a different tense, for example, *catch* becomes *caught*
letter patterns	groups of letters often found together in words, for example, 'igh', 'pre' or 'tion'
noun	a word for someone or something
past tense	the form of a verb showing something that has already happened
plural	a word for more than one of something, for example, *books, pencils* or *puppies*
prefix	a small group of letters added to the beginning of a word, for example 'un', 'dis' or 're'
present tense	the form of a verb showing something that is happening
pronoun	a word that replaces a noun, for example *him, her, it, they*
root word	the most basic form of a word before prefixes and suffixes have been added, for example, 'new' is the root word of 'renewing'
sentence	a group of words that makes sense standing alone
simile	an expression that describes something as being like something else, for example *the sun was as round as a golden coin*

singular	one of something, for example *dog*
stanza	poems can be divided into blocks of poetry called stanzas
suffix	a small group of letters added to the end of a word, for example, 'tion', 'ly' or 'ing'
synonym	a word with a meaning similar to another word, for example *smile, grin*
verb	an action or doing word
verb phrase	a small group of words that include a verb, for example, *am fishing* or *are working*
vowels	the letters a, e, i, o and u

11+ Study Guide

Essentials

- Don't worry too much about the level that you start at. Beginning with an easier book can help your confidence.
- Make sure you have the right equipment – you will need your pencils, an eraser, and a notebook.
- This book contains skills guidance and worked examples, but if you need more help with technique, the Bond Handbooks might also be useful to you.

Studying Effectively

1 Turn to the first topic and read the Key Skills box. You might want to read it a few times or with someone else to understand it properly or to underline key words.

2 Read the worked example a few times and make sure you understand it.

3 In your notebook, write down the topic heading and the worked example on a new page. This is for you to revise and remember. Once you have completed the final book, you will have a super-useful notebook that you can use in secondary school.

4 Now set a timer – a kitchen timer, a watch or phone with an alarm – for the timed section.

5 Work your way through the questions carefully. If you don't know the answer to something, draw a circle around the question number and take your best guess. This is important as you can find patterns if you make mistakes and it highlights where you need to consolidate.

6 Ask someone to mark the paper for you or mark it yourself and see where you made mistakes. Is there a common pattern? For every mistake, decide if it is not knowing the technique properly, not consolidating the technique enough or a loss of focus and label this next to each question using T = technique, C = consolidation, F = focus.

7 Have another go at the questions you made errors in to understand what you did wrong. If it is vocabulary problem, write down the word with its meaning / synonym / antonym at the back of your book so that you widen your vocabulary range.

Making Mistakes

Everyone makes mistakes and they are an important part of how we learn. The reason we practise before an exam is so that we can make those mistakes in a safe space rather than in the test itself and that way we can learn from them and make fewer mistakes when it really matters.

Remember that there is no such thing as a 'silly mistake'. You are not silly, and neither is your mistake. It is usually not understanding the technique, not consolidating the skill needed so that it is only partially remembered, or you have lost focus. Losing focus does not mean that you have done something bad, it just means that your attention was on something else. These tips can help:

Not Understanding the Technique:

- Go back to the learning section and reread the key skills box.
- Look at the worked example that you have in your notebook.
- Use the Bond Handbook for more support.

Not Consolidating Enough:

- It is amazing how much consolidation is needed by everyone so don't worry about doing lots of additional questions.
- Look at Bond online for some more questions to help you revise.
- Ask someone to test you on the technique.

Losing Focus:

- Make sure that you are not too tired, hungry, thirsty or distracted.
- Work out where you have made a mistake and break it down into sections. It might be that you focus on tricky division, but go too fast when it comes to addition. It might be that you read the comprehension extract, but you lost focus and misread it.
- Once you have identified the problem area, make sure that in new questions, you check yourself and focus carefully.

Common Problems

'I don't have time to study.'

Make sure that you have a timetable that is doable. If you have lots of activities that take up time, perhaps break your work up. The books all have timing sections so fit in smaller sections when you can. It's important to talk to your parent if you feel that you need more time for your 11+ work.

'I find it hard to complete my homework as I want to play instead.'

Motivation is difficult for most people. Don't completely stop all fun activities during the 11+ but get a balance. Key to this is a timetable so you know when, what and where to study. Make sure it is doable and build in something fun if you complete your homework for the day. Another tip is to write down your reasons for doing the 11+. It might be to keep your family happy, to get into a school your friends are going to, or even that the school is convenient. Ask yourself how important each reason is. Can you commit to the reasons you have? If so, keep remembering the reason and what will happen if you don't commit? Perhaps talk to your family so that they know how you feel.

'My friend is using different books to me.'

The Bond 11+ system covers English/Verbal Reasoning and Maths/Non-verbal reasoning/spatial awareness. Bond has had many decades of success in 11+ material. Many tutors will only use Bond for their pupils, and they get an exceptionally high pass rate. It doesn't mean that Bond is the only 11+ provider, so don't worry that your friend is using different material. What is important is that you are fully prepared for your CEM online exam, and you can have confidence in the Bond system.

'I'm scared of failing.'

It is natural to feel that. Remember that you cannot climb a mountain in one gigantic step. You need lots and lots of little steps to get to the top. The 11+ is like that. You can't sit down and learn everything straight away, but the little steps you take will lead you to the exam. Remember that every mistake can be identified and once you identify it, you may be able to understand it and solve the problem for next time. Mistakes are perfection in progress! If a selective school is the best learning environment for you, then you can work little and often through the books and then test papers leading up to the exam. If you find it too much and you are working at your full potential already, then maybe a school that is not selective will suit your learning better. There is no 'best school' and 'worst school' for everyone. It is the best school for an individual child. Do talk to someone about your feelings though as you need to feel supported.

'My friend has a tutor. Do I need one?'

Whether or not to have tutor depends on many different factors, including where your particular strengths and challenges lie, your own approach to learning, and whether your parents are comfortable with the costs involved. The Bond system is rigorous and aims to support every child with a range of books and learning materials. The Bond Handbooks can do the job of a tutor and many tutors also use the Bond books and Handbooks with their pupils. Bond has been providing 11+ material since the 1960s, helping thousands of pupils to pass their 11+ exams without having a tutor.

'I don't want to do the 11+ exam.'

This is a conversation to have with your family, but the best advice might be to follow the 11+ books anyway. They will teach you skills, techniques and methods that will give you self-confidence regardless of the secondary school you attend. No knowledge is a waste, and you will be keeping your options open.

There is more information on the Bond website. Bond has a Parent's Guide to the 11+ and there is a range of supportive printed and online material. See online for further details. ww.bond11plus.co.uk

Answers

Explanations in the main text of the book are referred to *by their page;* all other questions referred to can be found in the answer section.

Some questions will be answered in the children's own words. Answers to these questions are given in italics. Any answers that seem to be in line with these should be marked correct.

Learning Paper 1: Comprehension

1. *He was going to have a long sleep* (line 4).
2. *He was going to be at the very back of the queue* (lines 5–6).
3–6 Award one mark for each correct statement.
3. *He had to concentrate to count; he always ended up with paper cuts* (lines 15–17).
4. *It was a boring job; he ended up with sticky tape on him* (lines 21–3).
5. Any two of the following are acceptable: *he would get soapy and wet; they were messy eaters; he would get hot oats and bits of carrot on his hands* (lines 28–30).
6. *The boxes were heavy; he would feel both too hot and too cold* (lines 37–38).
7. *He was turning to look for Noel Claus; he spotted a movement behind the Christmas tree* (lines 39–40).
8. *He would make them feel more comfortable before their long travels* (line 50).
9. Award one mark for each of the following: **a shovel, a brush, a bucket** (line 51).
10. *The reindeer dung would be put into the Christmas garden compost heap to help provide some lovely roses in the summer.* (lines 52–53).
11. Any two of the following: **horrified, dismay** or **worst job** (lines 54–55). 'Horrified' means filled with horror and very shocked and 'dismay' means upset and distress.
12. a *slowly, in a relaxed and calm way*
    b *keen or enthusiastic, wanting to do or have something*
    c *extremely happy, feeling great joy or excitement*
    d *distress, a feeling of shock or alarm*
13. Any three of the following reasons: *the word is repeated; two of them are written in block capital letters; one of them is written in bold type; the words get larger.*

Learning Paper 2: Words in Context

1. c **busy** 'Busy' means active, with a lot to do.
2. a **strict** 'Strict' means stern or firm.
3. b **century** A decade is ten years and a millennium is one thousand years; a kilometre is used to measure length and a dozen is twelve.
4. a **medicine** The sentence describes a doctor prescribing something, so 'medicine' makes the most sense.
5. a **group** All the other words describe groups of animals.
6. e **naughty** The dog is being described as doing something mischievous so this is the most appropriate word.
7. b **imagine** The sentence is describing what something would be like, so 'remember' will not work in this sentence; only 'imagine' would.
8. c **variety** A group of different fruits is described in the sentence, so 'variety' is the most appropriate answer.
9. c **separate** In cooking, separating the egg white means removing it from the yolk.
10. a **promise** A promise is an oath, when someone gives their word.
11. d **sometimes** Both words mean from time to time or once in a while.
12. a **protect** Both words mean to defend.
13. c **strange** Both words mean unusual.
14. b **maybe** Both words mean possibly.
15. a **so** Both words mean 'for that reason'.

Learning Paper 3: Missing Letters

1–9 Award 1 mark for both correct words.
1. **ina** (ord<u>ina</u>ry); **pri** (<u>pri</u>ncess)
2. **ish** (pun<u>ish</u>ed); **eys** (donk<u>eys</u>)
3. **won** (<u>won</u>derful); **gin** (brin<u>gin</u>g)
4. **che** (tea<u>che</u>rs); **kin** (stoc<u>kin</u>gs)
5. **erh** (p<u>erh</u>aps); **pul** (<u>pul</u>ar)
6. **ain** (r<u>ain</u>bow); **hic** (<u>chic</u>ken)
7. **und** (<u>und</u>erstood); **owe** (borr<u>owe</u>d)
8. **eti** (som<u>eti</u>mes); **whe** (any<u>whe</u>re)
9. **ing** (darl<u>ing</u>); **rew** (fi<u>rew</u>ork)
10. **HEM** (t<u>hem</u>selves)
11. **TIN** (wri<u>tin</u>g)
12. **LOW** (b<u>low</u>ing)
13. **HAD** (s<u>had</u>ows)
14. **DIN** (pud<u>din</u>g)
15. **RIG** (b<u>rig</u>htest)

Learning Paper 4: Vocabulary

1–9 Two words must be underlined for 1 mark.
1. **kitten, puppy** All the other words are adult, not baby, animals.
2. **fingers, toes** All the other words are parts of the face.
3. **rice, pasta** All the other words are things you put food on or in.
4. **ears, legs** All the other words are things you do.
5. **gold, silver** All the other words are types of jewellery.
6. **cottage, house** 'Cottage' and 'house' are buildings people live in; all the other words are areas people live in.
7. **forest, woods** All the other words are flowers.
8. **butterfly, moth** All the other words are minibeasts that cannot fly.
9. **nostrils, lips** All the other words are related to the eye.
10. **bright** 'Bright' can mean smart and describe a glowing light.
11. **steps** 'Steps' can be a verb describing movement ('she steps'); 'steps' are also something you walk up to reach a higher level.

12 **ring** 'Ring' can mean to call and speak to someone on a phone; it can also mean a round shape.
13 **hard** 'Hard' can mean firm and solid; it can also mean challenging.
14 **mean** To be mean is to be unkind; it can also mean tight-fisted, not generous.

Learning Paper 5: Grammar 1

1 **house** The letter 's' just needs to be removed.
2 **church** 'es' has been added as the word ends in the letters 'ch'.
3 **child** This is an irregular plural noun, so 's' or 'es' has not been added as it is in other words. Instead, one or more of the letters change.
4 **scarf** When 'es' is removed, the last letter is 'v', so this must have been changed from an 'f'.
5 **puppy** When 'es' is removed, the last letter is 'i', so this must have been changed from an 'y'.
6 **fly** Refer to question 5.
7 **lunch** Refer to question 2.
8 **cinema** There are trapeze artists in a circus.
9 **leg** The little dog wagged his tail.
10 **bakery** The library had no books about the Vikings.
11 **handbag** The queen wore her gold crown.
12 **divide** Three add two makes five.
13 **but**
14 **because**
15 **or**
16 **so**
17 **yet**

Learning Paper 6: Antonyms and Synonyms

1–5 Award one mark for each word.
1 **chilly, freezing, icy** All three words mean cold.
2 **safe, harmless** 'Dangerous' means hazardous, whereas these two words mean secure and free from risk.
3 **yell, scream, howl** All three words mean a loud noise made with the voice.
4 **clean, spotless, sparkling** 'Dirty' means filthy, whereas these three words mean cleansed or polished.
5 **claw, nail** All words describe the curved part at the end of a limb.
6–10 Award one mark for each word.
6 **loss, defeat** A win is a victory, whereas these words mean failure.
7 **build, make, create** 'Destroy' means to pull something apart, whereas these words mean to put something together.
8 **reveal, expose** To 'hide' means to conceal, whereas these words mean to show.
9 **fear, dread, horror, fright** All these words describe a feeling of alarm or being scared.
10 **mild, kind, soft** All these words mean tender.
11 tr<u>ouse</u>rs
12 b<u>urni</u>ng
13 wh<u>ole</u>
14 di<u>vide</u>
15 n<u>oi</u>se
16 **irrelevant** 'Important' describes something that is significant and necessary, whereas 'irrelevant' means unnecessary or unconnected.

17 **part** 'Whole' describes something that is complete, whereas a part is a section of something.
18 **rarely** If something happens often it happens quite a lot, whereas 'rarely' means it hardly ever happens.
19 **question** A question is something that is asked, whereas an answer is a response to something that is asked.
20 **drop** To 'catch' something means to grab and hold something that has been thrown, whereas to 'drop' means to let go of something so it falls.

Learning Paper 7: Grammar 2

1 **red (read)** 'Red' is a colour; 'read' is the past tense of 'read' and, although they are spelled the same, they are pronounced differently.
2 **plaice (place)** 'Plaice' is a type of fish; 'place' is a position or area.
3 **new (knew)** 'New' means recent or fresh; 'knew' is the past tense of 'know'.
4 **wear (where)** To 'wear' means to have items of clothing on; 'where' describes something in or at a certain place.
5 **two (to, too)** 'To' is used to describe direction or action to a person or place; 'too' means more than is necessary or in addition; and 'two' is a number.
6 **ate (eight)** 'Ate' is the past tense of eat; 'eight' is a number.
7 **following** The root word 'follow' has the letter 'l' doubled, so this word should have the same.
8 **strawberries** The root word is 'strawberry' so the 'r' should be doubled. The 'y' at the end of the word should change to 'i' before 'es' is added.
9 **apples** The 'e' and 'l' are the wrong way round.
10 **banana** Two 'n's and one 'a' need to be removed.
11 **scoops** The 'w' needs to be removed.
12 **vanilla** One 'n' and the 'r' at the end need to be removed. The 'l' needs to be doubled.
13 **fruit** The 'ute' part of the word should be spelled 'uit'.
14 **cream** The 'ee' part of the word should be spelled 'ea'.
15–20 Answers should use the smallest number of words possible, so 'I ate' rather than 'I was eating.'
15 **I rode my bike.**
16 **Megan spoke to Grandma.**
17 **Liam washed his hair.**
18 **We ran in the race.**
19 **Katie wrote in her diary.**
20 **My mum drove her new car.**

Learning Paper 8: Cloze

1 **lived**
2 **animals**
3 **squirrel**
4 **finding**
5 **hopped**
6 **twitching**
7 **vixen**
8 **hunted**
9 **emerged**
10 **undergrowth**
11 **distance**

12 planets
13 remember
14 telescope
15 looking

Curveball Questions 1

1 a **lion** A lion is often called the 'king of the jungle', and it roars.
2 **packed lunch** As it mentions not going hungry, it must be food and packed lunches are taken on trips. (Answers such as sandwiches are also acceptable.)
3 **orange** (lemon, lime) As it mentions 'juice', it must be from a fruit; the only colour that is also a fruit is orange. Children may say lemon and lime and these answers should also be accepted.
4 **hedgehog** Hedgehogs are nocturnal animals that curl into a ball to protect themselves.
5 *He has broken his leg. He did this playing rugby.* His friends are signing the plaster cast on his leg, so he must have broken it. As it says he will 'be more careful next time he plays rugby', it suggests this is how he did it.
6 *She is feeling excited. It is Friday.* We can tell she is excited as it mentions that she 'couldn't wait for school to finish' and we feel like this when we are looking forward to, or are excited about, something happening. It tells us it is a school day, but not a school day tomorrow. Therefore it must be Friday.
7 *She is fishing. She is excited because she has just caught a fish.* We know she is fishing because she is at a river and the words 'line', 'rod' and 'reel' are included. When an angler catches a fish, they 'reel it in', so she must have caught a fish.

8–11

	Red collar	White paws	Blue collar	Black paws
Topsy	✓	✓		
Flopsy			✓	✓
Tipsy	✓			✓
Dipsy		✓	✓	

8 Tipsy
9 Topsy
10 Dipsy
11 Flopsy

Mixed Paper 1

1 Award 1 mark for each of the following: **Pals** (in the title), **mates** (line 8), **buddy** (line 16).
2 *It has a lot of teeth which are tightly packed together and make its mouth look like a parrot's beak* (lines 2–3).
3 *The mucus layer is brightly coloured* (lines 5–6).
4 Award one mark for each of the following: *it forms a mucus layer at night; the layer is to protect it* (line 5).
5 Award one mark for each of the following: *The goby cleans away the food that is stuck to the teeth of the parrotfish; it gobbles up the rotten skin to keep the parrotfish healthy* (lines 17–19).
6 **As clean as a new pin**
7 Award one mark for each correct definition:
   a *eat, chew, gobble, nibble*
   b *stomach, belly*
   c *best, close, tight, strong*
8 Award two marks for any two of the following: *they need each other; the parrotfish needs the goby to keep it healthy and clean; the goby needs the parrotfish to provide it with food so that it doesn't have to hunt for food.*
9–19 Refer to pages 20–22 on Grammar.
   9 **feet** You need to wash your hands before making sandwiches.
   10 **shed** We planted a rose bush in the garden.
   11 **wood** Jeans are often made from denim.
   12 **space** The bus to town was running late.
   13 **coaches** The fishermen returned with full boats.
   14 **but**
   15 **because**
   16 **so**
   17 **or**
   18 **Although**
   19 **if**
20–23 Refer to pages 13–15 on Words in Context.
   20 c **mix** Both words mean to combine or put together.
   21 b **line** Both words describe people standing one after another in a row.
   22 d **job** Both words mean an activity that someone does to earn money.
   23 a **area** Both words mean a certain part of a place.
24–28 Refer to pages 30–31 on Grammar.
   24 **cushion** The letter 's' just needs to be removed.
   25 **purse** The letter 's' just needs to be removed.
   26 **thief** When 'es' is removed, the last letter is 'v', so this must have been changed from an 'f'.
   27 **party** When 'es' is removed, the last letter is 'i', so this must have been changed from a 'y'.
   28 **mouse** This is an irregular plural noun, so 's' or 'es' has not been added as it is in other words. Instead, one or more of the letters change.
29–33 Refer to pages 29–30 on Cloze questions.
   29 **bear**
   30 **ears**
   31 **climb**
   32 **eat**
   33 **hours**

Mixed Paper 2

1 Bella draws a picture.
2 Simon climbs the ladder.
3 The dog sleeps in his basket.
4 Kayleigh drives the tractor.
5 Erica flies a kite.
6 Pneuma thinks about a holiday.
7–14 Refer to pages 27–29 on Grammar.
   7 **peaceful** The root word is 'peace' and the suffix 'ful' is added.
   8 **quiet** 'ei' must be changed to 'ie' and the 'e' at the end of the word must be removed.
   9 **themselves** The singular version of this word is 'themself'. The 'f' changes to a 'v', and 'es' is added to make it plural.

Mixed Papers 2–4

10. **coloured** The root word is 'colour' and the suffix 'ed' is added.
11. **insects** The 'ext' part of the word should be spelled 'ect'.
12. **actually** The root word is 'actual' and the suffix 'ly' is added.
13. **habitat** Although this word sounds as though the letters should be doubled, there should only be single 'b's and 't's and this spelling needs to be learnt separately.
14. **nature** The 'y' needs to be removed and 'chur' should be spelled 'ture'.
15. **clothed** Both words mean to wear clothes.
16. **middle** Both words mean the innermost part of something.
17. **idea** Both words mean something imagined in the mind.
18. **own** Both words mean to have.
19. **maybe** Both words mean almost certain, but not definite.
20–25. Refer to pages 18–19 on Vocabulary.
20. **ball** A ball is a piece of sports equipment; it is also an event where dancing takes place.
21. **pen** A pen is something pigs live in; it is also something you can write with.
22. **stick** To 'stick' means to paste and fasten; a stick is also a long, thin object.
23. **sweet** 'Sweet' means charming; a sweet is a dish eaten at the end of a meal.
24. **tablet** A tablet is something taken as medicine; it is also a small, portable computer.
25. **upset** To 'upset' means to knock over; 'upset' also means unhappy.

Curveball Questions 2

26. Award one mark for either of the following: *to conquer means to win; he was a conqueror as he won the battle of Hastings* (line 1).
27. *So that people know which king or queen we mean* (lines 3–5).
28. **Henry II** (line 7)
29. **1455** (lines 12–13)
30. **Henry VI** (line 11)
31. **12 years old** (line 15)
32. **three** (lines 20–21)
33. **Lady Jane Grey** (lines 23–24)
34. **Charles II** (line 25)
35. **five years** (line 27–28)
36. **the Tudor period** or **1485–1603** (line 22)
37. **the Hanoverian period** or **1714–1901** (lines 33–34)
38. **Queen Victoria** (line 31)
39. Award one mark for either of the following: *Queen Anne died without leaving any children*; *the German George I was her closest Protestant relative* (lines 32–33).
40. *There was an anti-German feeling because of the First World War, and Windsor sounded more English* (line 38).

Mixed Paper 3

1. a **teddy bear** (line 20)
2. Award three marks for any three of the following: *the lines are short*; *each line begins with a capital letter*; *the writing is broken into stanzas* ('verses' or 'sections' instead of stanzas is acceptable); *there are rhyming words at the ends of lines, in a pattern*.
3. Award one mark for each of the following: **a camp site** (lines 9–10), **a castle**, **the beach**, **a hilltop zoo** (lines 13–14).
4. Award one mark for any of the following: **we** (a homophone of 'wee', which means little); **sea** (a homophone of 'see' which means to view); **heard** (a homophone of 'herd', which is a group of animals, such as cows); **waves** (a homophone of 'waives', which means gives up or rejects); **be** (a homophone of 'bee', a winged insect).
5. **Charlie is my favourite friend** (lines 1 and 19).
6. Award three marks for any three of the following: *they go everywhere together* (line 2); *he makes the writer laugh* (line 3); *he makes the writer smile* (line 3); *he always smiles* (line 6); *he is always trying to cheer the writer up* (line 7); *they laugh so much together* (line 15).
7. **He is** 'He's' is a contraction of 'he is' (line 20).
8–14. Refer to pages 16–17 on Missing Letters.
8. **ARK** (d<u>ark</u>er)
9. **EAR** (l<u>ear</u>nt)
10. **ROW** (bor<u>row</u>ed)
11. **THE** (ra<u>the</u>r)
12. **URN** (t<u>urn</u>ips)
13. **RAN** (st<u>ran</u>gers)
14. **TIN** (ska<u>tin</u>g)
15–20. Refer to pages 18–19 on Vocabulary. Two words must be underlined for 1 mark.
15. **huge, big** All the other words mean small.
16. **television, radio** All the others are printed on paper.
17. **boiling, hot** All the other words mean chilly.
18. **hand, elbow** All the others are internal organs.
19. **driver, passenger** All the others are vehicles.
20. **bread, cake** All the others are dairy products.
21–27. Refer to pages 24–27 on Antonyms and Synonyms.
21. c<u>l</u>ean
22. poo<u>r</u>ly
23. war<u>m</u>th
24. <u>l</u>arge
25. hi<u>g</u>h
26. <u>f</u>ashion
27. s<u>n</u>ip
28–33. Refer to pages 27–29 on Grammar.
28. **wring** (homophone: ring) To 'wring' means to squeeze liquid out of something; a 'ring' is a round shape or a piece of jewellery.
29. **sight** (homophone: site) 'Sight' is vision; a 'site' is an area of ground.
30. **hair** (homophone: hare) 'Hair' are strands that are found on the head; a 'hare' is an animal.
31. **their** (homophones: there, they're) 'Their' is used to show something belongs to someone; 'there' refers to a place or position; and 'they're' is the shortened form of 'they are'.
32. **horse** (homophone: hoarse) A 'horse' is an animal; 'hoarse' describes a rough-sounding voice.
33. **break** (homophone: brake) 'Break' means to separate into pieces; a 'brake' is used to stop a vehicle.

Mixed Paper 4

1–6 Refer to pages 23–26 on Antonyms and Synonyms.
1. **deliberate** 'Accidental' means not done on purpose, whereas 'deliberate' means done on purpose.
2. **unsure** 'Certain' means absolutely confident about something, whereas 'unsure' means doubtful.
3. **shrink** 'Increase' means to become larger, whereas 'shrink' means to become smaller.
4. **huge** 'Minute' means very small, whereas 'huge' means very large.
5. **unusual** 'Ordinary' means normal, whereas 'unusual' means abnormal.

6–10 Award one mark for each correct word.
6. **poor**, **world** It cannot be 'pour' as this means to carefully tip liquid; it cannot be 'whirled' as this means quickly spun around.
7. **rain**, **sun** It cannot be 'rein' as this is part of a horse's harness; it cannot be 'son' as this means the male child of parents.
8. **their**, **be** It cannot be 'there' as this refers to a place or position; it cannot be 'bee' this is a winged insect.
9. **die**, **needs** It cannot be 'dye' as this is used to change something's colour; it cannot be 'knead' as this means to shape and squeeze with the hands.
10. **know**, **for** It cannot be 'no' as this means the opposite of 'yes'; it cannot be 'four' as this is a number.
11. **raise**, **save** It cannot be 'rays' as these are beams of light; it cannot be 'safe' as this describes something that *is* 'free from harm', not *to* 'free from harm'.

21–24 Refer to pages 20–22 on Grammar.
21. **hurricane** The pretty flowers bobbed gently in the breeze.
22. **lemon** Our new car is as red as a cherry.
23. **displaying** Robert loved working at the museum.
24. **enemies** The two children were the best of friends.
25. **magic** The suffixes 'al' and 'ly' have been added: magic + al + ly.
26. **beauty** As the root word ends in a 'y', this letter changes to an 'i' when the suffix 'ful' is added.
27. **silly** Refer to question 26.
28. **clever** The suffix 'est' has been added: clever + est.
29. **small** The suffix 'er' has been added: small + er.

30–34 Refer to pages 18–19 on Vocabulary. Two words must be underlined for one mark.
30. **fifteen, nineteen** All the other words are multiples of ten.
31. **shape, angle** All the other words are 2D shapes.
32. **leaves, snow** All the other words are seasons.
33. **one, single** All the other words mean two.
34. **fleece, jacket** All the other words are fastenings.

35–38 Refer to pages 16–17 on Missing Letters. Award one mark for both correct words.
35. **ybi** (lad<u>ybi</u>rd); **ict** (d<u>ict</u>ionary)
36. **aug** (n<u>aug</u>hty); **ter** (li<u>ter</u>acy)
37. **cro** (<u>cro</u>wded); **eri** (show<u>eri</u>ng)
38. **ass** (<u>ass</u>embly); **ona** (lem<u>ona</u>de)

39–44 Refer to pages 31–32 on Cloze questions.
39. **birthday**
40. **ready**
41. **neighbour**
42. **games**
43. **decorations**
44. **arrived**

Curveball Questions 2

1. a A corridor or a walkway.
   b A small island.
   c The shortened form of the words 'I will'.
2. a A word used to show who does something or another word for 'next to'.
   b Spoken when you leave somebody.
   c Get something by paying money.
3. a Used to describe a place or position.
   b Used to describe something that belongs to a person or group of people.
   c The shortened form of the words 'they are'.
4. a Another word for 'so that' or 'toward'.
   b Another word for 'as well'.
   c The number that comes after one.
5. a A tiny hole in the skin.
   b To carefully tip liquid.
   c Low quality or having no money.
6. a A tarmac track that cars drive on.
   b The past tense of 'ride'.
   c Moved a boat with oars.
7. **owl**, **food**
8. **looked**, **screeching**
9. **little**, **tasty**
10. **carefully**, **loudly**

Test Paper 1

1. Award one mark for either of the following: magazine or comic. Award a further three marks for any three of the following: It is written in columns. (1) It states that the next edition can be bought from a newsagents. (1) It references pages 'on page 24'. (1) There is a crossword to fill in and post off. (1) There is a variety of writing styles and information. (1)
2. **19th May** This is the date shown for 'Biscuits & Cookies'.
3. *Decorated cakes including wedding and birthday cakes.*
4. **8th July**
5. **Samuel (Sammy) Jacobson**
6. *Harder fruit takes longer to cook than softer fruit.*
7. **225 g** 25 g for the filling and 200 g for the topping.
8. a **rough** Both words describe a lumpy texture.
   b **contestants** Both words mean people who take part in a competition.
   c **version** Both words describe someone's individual approach to something.
9. Award one mark for each of the following: **fling, chuck, toss, pop**

10–14 Refer to pages 20–22 on Grammar.
10. **so**
11. **because**
12. **and**
13. **but**
14. **or**

15–21 Refer to pages 16–17 on Missing Letters.
 15 **PAD** (s<u>pad</u>es)
 16 **VAT** (pri<u>vat</u>e)
 17 **POT** (s<u>pot</u>ted)
 18 **ASK** (b<u>ask</u>et)
 19 **TEN** (mit<u>ten</u>s)
 20 **PIG** (<u>pig</u>eons)
 21 **AND** (h<u>and</u>bag)
22–25 Refer to pages 23–26 on Antonyms and Synonyms. Award one mark for each word.
 22 **reign, rule, govern** All words mean to be in charge of.
 23 **unusual, different, odd, strange** 'Ordinary' means normal, whereas all these words mean abnormal.
 24 **undecided, unsure** All these words mean doubtful.
 25 **caught, trapped** 'Free' means loose and able to do as one pleases, whereas these words mean captured or snared.
26–31 Refer to pages 28–29 on Grammar.
 26 **boxes**
 27 **copies**
 28 **donkeys**
 29 **heroes**
 30 **leaves**
 31 **teeth**
 32 **mice**
33–35 Refer to pages 13–15 on Words in Context.
 33 a **b sunset** Although all the words mean parts of the day, only 'sunset' and 'dusk' mean the evening time.
    b **a perfume** Both words describe a pleasant smell.
 34 a **c jumped** Both words mean sprang upwards.
    b **d unknowing** Both words mean unwary.
 35 a **c ongoing** Both words mean going on without a break.
    b **a stopping** Both words mean coming to a halt.
36–42 Refer to pages 28–29 on Grammar. Answers should use the smallest number of words possible, so 'I ate' rather than 'I was eating.'
 36 **We watched a film.**
 37 **Simona played football with her friends.**
 38 **Mei-Lin practised for her piano exam.**
 39 **I made a model of a ship.**
 40 **She drew a picture of a horse.**
 41 **Thea read her book.** Although pronounced differently, the present and past tense of 'read' are spelled the same.
 42 **We had a picnic.**
 43 **century** Although this word sounds as though an 'a' should be inserted, this needs to be removed and the spelling needs to be learnt separately.
 44 **built** This word has a silent 'u' and this spelling needs to be learnt separately.
 45 **history** The letters 'er' and 'or' sound the same in some words and, to know which one to use on particular words, these spellings have to be learnt individually.
 46 **library** This has two r's when spelled correctly. The letters 'a' and 'r' at the end of the word are unstressed, which means they are barely pronounced.
 47 **special** When a word ends in a 'shul' sound, the letters 'cial' or 'tial' are placed at the end and these spellings have to be learnt individually.
48–52 Refer to pages 28–29 on Grammar.
 48 **bored (board)** To be 'bored' means to feel fed up because of not doing anything; a board is a flat piece of wood.
 49 **you (ewe, yew)** 'You' is the opposite of 'I' or 'me'; a ewe is a female sheep; yew is a type of tree.
 50 **him (hymn)** The pronoun 'him' is used when talking about a male person; a hymn is a religious song.
 51 **weight (wait)** The weight of something is how heavy it is; to 'wait' means to stay in a place until something happens.
 52 **flower (flour)** A flower is part of a plant; flour is a grain that has been ground down for cooking.

Test Paper 2

1–6 Refer to pages 23–26 on Antonyms and Synonyms.
 1 **appear** To 'disappear' means to go out of sight, whereas 'appear' means to come into sight.
 2 **late** 'Early' means before an expected time, whereas 'late' means after an expected time.
 3 **easy** 'Difficult' means hard, whereas 'easy' means simple.
 4 **unequal** 'Regular' means not varied, whereas 'uneven' means varying.
 5 **unlikely** If something is possible there is a good chance it could happen, whereas 'unlikely' means there is a small chance it could happen.
 6 **artificial** 'Natural' means made by nature, whereas 'artificial' means man-made.
7–10 Refer to pages 16–17 on Missing Letters.
 7 **OWE** (h<u>owe</u>ver)
 8 **ASS** (gl<u>ass</u>es)
 9 **RAN** (b<u>ran</u>ches)
 10 **TEE** (thir<u>tee</u>n)
11–21 Refer to pages 23–26 on Antonyms and Synonyms. Award one mark for each word on questions 11–14.
 11 **broken, ruined, wrecked** All three words describe something that has been damaged, sometimes beyond repair.
 12 **tired, sleepy, dozy, drowsy** 'Energetic' means alert and active; the other words mean lacking in energy.
 13 **easy, simple** 'Difficult' means hard; the other words mean straightforward and uncomplicated.
 14 **cloth, material** All words are textiles.
 15 ca<u>rton</u>
 16 bla<u>ze</u>
 17 <u>b</u>east
 18 <u>number</u>
 19 in<u>j</u>ury
 20 sca<u>red</u>
 21 un<u>clean</u>
22–25 Refer to pages 13–15 on Words in Context.
 22 a **shut** In this context, both words mean to finish business for the day.
 23 c **nice** Both words mean lovely and good.
 24 c **white** Both words mean very light in colour.

25 **b price** Both words mean the money asked for or paid for something.
26–34 Refer to Mixed Paper 4 questions 16–20 on Root Words.
26 **sit** The prefix 're' and the suffix 'ing' have been added; the letter 't' is doubled as the root word ends in a single vowel, followed by a single consonant.
27 **travel** The suffix 'ing' has been added; refer to question 30.
28 **possible** The prefix 'im' and the suffix 'ly' have been added; the letters 'le' are removed before the suffix is added.
29 **act** The prefix 'in' and the suffix 'ive' have been added.
30 **settle** The prefix 'un' and the suffix 'ed' have been added; the 'e' is removed before the suffix is added.
31–38 Refer to pages 20–22 on Grammar.
31 **glass** The letters 'es' just need to be removed.
32 **goddess** The letters 'e s' just need to be removed.
33 **piglet** The letter 's' just needs to be removed.
34 **pony** When 'es' is removed, the last letter is 'i', so this must have been changed from a 'y'.
35 **fairy** Refer to question 10.
36 **person** This is an irregular plural noun, so 's' or 'es' has not been added as it is in other words. Instead, one or more of the letters change.
37 **monkey** The letter 's' just needs to be removed.
38 **knife** When 'es' is removed, the last letter is 'v', so this must have been changed from an 'f'.
39 **d in the middle of the pile of comics** (lines 5–6)
40 **b Gladys** She has written her own address at the top of the letter (lines 10–12).
41 **d There was not enough space; e Al wouldn't be able to play football** (lines 28–29).
42 **b Dad wanted a rest from packing; d It was quite close by** (lines 40–42)
43 **d upset** She was shocked by what he found (line 56).
44 **c She was expecting flowers and trees** She was imagining what it would look like and thought he would see an orangery and a sunken garden (lines 43–45) or a park (line 46–47).
45 a **collection** Both words mean a hoard.
   b **colourful** Both words mean bright.
   c **restoring** Both words mean repairing and revamping.
46 **b jealous as he didn't want to share the garden** Al was not sure he wanted to share the park with anyone (lines 47–48).
47–52 Refer to pages 23–26 on Antonyms and Synonyms.
47 **leave** 'Arrive' means to come, whereas 'leave' means to go.
48 **doubt** To 'believe' means to accept something is true, whereas to 'doubt' means to be unsure.
49 **old** Something that is fresh is new and modern, whereas something that is old is from a long time ago.
50 **similar** 'Opposite' means completely different, whereas 'similar' means alike.
51 **bored** 'Bored' means fed up with doing an activity, whereas 'interested' means curious and focused.
52 **begin** 'Begin' means to start, whereas 'end' means to finish.
53–59 Refer to pages 18–19 on Vocabulary.
53 **top** A top is a piece of clothing worn on the upper part of the body; it is also a cover that can be removed from the top of a bottle.
54 **wind** Wind is the movement of air; to 'wind' (pronounced differently) means to move something in a circular direction.
55 **train** To 'train' means to educate; a train is a form of transport.
56 **minute** A minute is a unit of time; 'minute' (pronounced differently) means very small.
57 **spring** To 'spring' means to bob or bounce upwards; spring is one of the seasons.
58 **saw** 'Saw' is the past tense of 'see'; it also means to cut something by moving a blade back and forth.
59 **trip** To 'trip' means to fall or stumble over something; a trip is also a visit or journey.

Notes